ROY WEBB'S
REDDITCH

This book is dedicated to my parents
Sydney and Annie Webb.

It is for my brother Roy and in memory of
my sisters Doreen and Mary.

ROY WEBB'S
REDDITCH
THEN & NOW

– CONSERVATION FOR OUR TIME –

Tina Emily Webb-Moore

HISTORY INTO PRINT

HISTORY INTO PRINT
56 Alcester Road,
Studley,
Warwickshire,
B80 7LG
www.history-into-print.com

Published by History Into Print 2014

ISBN: 978-1-85858-347-1

Printed and bound in Great Britain
by MWL Print Group.

Contents

List of Illustrations

Back Cover
Roy Webb age 18.

Introduction
Our parents Sidney Webb with his wife Annie and Roy 1922.

Chapter 1
Roy with our mother and sisters Doreen and Mary 1928.
Bluebells in Malvern Worcestershire © T Kidger.
First leaves of spring 2011 © E Moore.

Chapter 2
Brian's Garden in Hanley Swan, Worcestershire © B Skeys.
Roy, 7 years old.
1st Prize at Hanley Swan Village Show, Worcestershire © Rebecca.
2nd Prize at Hanley Swan Village Show, Worcestershire © Louise.
Northern Pike (known as pike in Britain) Courtesy U.S. Fish and Wildlife Service.
Ellen Elizabeth Gazey with grandson Gerald, in front of 253 Beoley Road circa
    1930/31.
Ellen in Gazey Fields wearing her Sunday Apron.

Chapter 4
Roy Webb c 1940.
Coventry Cathedral:
    Ruined Cathedral (St Michael's) morning of 15th November 1940.
    Inside St Michael's Church (Coventry Cathedral) c 1910.
    June 2006 Showing new cathedral and ruins of old cathedral.
Rape field view from Malvern Hills © E Moore.
My brother with his wife Irene and daughter Katrina 1947.

Chapter 5
Golden Chain (Laburnum) © B Skeys.

Chapter 6
Memorial for James Davies, St Leonard's Church yard, Beoley © B.K. Watkins.
James Henry Styler with his wife Henrietta.

St Leonard's Church yard, Beoley, © B.K. Watkins.
Brian's White Garden © B Skeys.
Irene M Webb with school children.
St George's Church with author in the foreground – 2012 © E Moore.
Market Place Redditch – old postcard.
Peacock butterfly © B Skeys.
Lilac © B Skeys.
Bee on Sedum flowers © B Skeys.

Chapter 8
Andy Harvey Song Thrush (rspb-images.com) copyright protected.
Chris Gomersall Yellow Hammer (rspb-images.com) copyright protected.
Gold finches Brian's garden in January 2013 © B Skeys.
Wild Geranium © E Moore.
Lapwing (peewit) Andy Hay (rspb-images.com) copyright protected.
The Grey Heron © Photograph by Richard Newton.
Blue tit © Photograph by Richard Newton.
Sparrow Ray Kennedy (rspb-images.com) copyright protected.
Kestrel © Richard Newton.
Roy Webb's Cherry tree.

Chapter 9
Conservation State of Nature RSPB ©.
Primular Vulgaris © B Skeys.
Daffodils © B Skeys.
Yellow Rattle or Cockscomb (Rhinanthus minor) © B Skeys.
St Leonard's Church, Beoley © B.K. Watkins.
Guelder Rose © B Skeys.
Vibumum Opulus – Guelder Rose © B Skeys.
My brother with our mother.
Roy gathering flowers in the lane.
Caterpillar of Mullein Moth on Verbascum © B Skeys.
North American Grey Squirrel with white tipped tail photograph
    © E.F. Vozenilek.
Dandelion © E Moore.
Thistle flowers © B Skeys.

Addendum: Illustrations

Family photograph circa 1929 taken in the garden of 253 Beoley Road, shows Sarah Jane (Jin) with her hands on the shoulders of Mary Kathleen, with Mary's brother Tom on her right and Ellen Elizabeth Anne (Nell) standing behind him.

Last known photograph of Ellen Elizabeth Gazey circa 1940/42 with her dogs Lassie the Old English Sheep dog on the left, and Tangee the Terrier on the right.

"Dol" the carthorse standing at the junction of 223 Beoley Road and Prospect Road where Joseph George Gazey lived (undated).

Children playing in the waters of The Brook (River Arrow) at the bottom of Beoley Road, Redditch (undated).

Ellen Elizabeth Gazey with her grandsons Edward (Ted) on the right and Gerald (sons of Joseph George) with her ducklings circa 1930/31.

"Ordnance Survey" Map 1887 showing the River Arrow, Beoley Lane, "Gazey Fields" and Beoley Mill Cottages, Redditch, courtesy of Forge Mill Needle Museum, Redditch, Worcestershire, England.

Quotations inserted by Author

Chapter 3
William Shakespeare, "Romeo and Juliet"
(23.04.1564 – 23.04.1616)

Chapter 4
Leo Tolstoy, "War and Peace"
(11.09.1828 – 20.11.1910)

Chapter 6
Places
Henry James, "Three things in human life are important"
(15.04.1843 – 28.02.1916)

Chapter 7
Winston Churchill, "All the great things are simple"
(30.11.1874 – 14.01.1965)

Chapter 9
J.R.R. Tolkien, "Faerie contains many things besides elves and fays"
(03.01.1892 – 02.09.1973)

Author unknown, An Old Proverb about Daisies

Claude Debussy, "There is nothing is more musical than a sunset"
(22.08.1862 – 25.03.1918)

Epilogue
John Muir, "Keep close to Nature's Heart"
(21.04.1838 – 24.12.1914)

Roy Webb

MY BROTHER Roy Webb, son of Sydney Webb and his wife Annie (nee Styler), was born in Redditch on 29th June 1921. He lived with his parents and sisters in Beoley Road, Redditch, and attended St Stephen's Boys' School Redditch and then Redditch County High School (now Trinity High School). He excelled academically achieving the University of Oxford, Higher School Certificate in History, English, French (oral and written) and Economics. He recalls visiting his grandmother Prudence Styler, who lived in Other Road near Redditch County High School, during the school lunch break, and writes that he adored her. He subsequently passed the Civil Service examination. Between leaving school and volunteering to serve in the army in the Second World War he was actively involved in the Redditch Poetry Circle later the Redditch Society. After serving in the Second World War he married Irene Muriel Gay (born in Norfolk) 31st August 1946, at St Peter's Church, Ipsley. They had one daughter Katrina Jennifer. He worked for local government and apart from his professional duties wrote for their branch magazine. Later he worked in private business. He enjoyed walking from his home to visit our parents, where he would have long and animated conversations with our father and also supported his mother. He attended St Peter's Church, Ipsley and St George's Church, Redditch.

His daughter Katrina recalls,

> *"My father loved going to the theatre in his lifetime. I used to hear about his visits to the Old Rep Theatre in Birmingham and the Shakespeare Theatre in Stratford upon Avon especially. He was I would say obsessed with Shakespeare in my memories of him. He was always quoting him. He also loved the works of Charles Dickens and would quote a lot from him also!! My father would also quote constantly from classical poets – to mind: Tennyson, Wordsworth, Shelley – to name a few. Of course my father had a classic education and he was in his element."*

Roy's other passion, as can be seen from the early photographs taken of him and his writing was everything that represented nature. The long walks that he took together with his clear mind enabled him to make the accurate and colourful reports about birds, flora and fauna which are presented here for all to enjoy. His love of the local area was the inspiration for the many letters that he wrote, and also drove his concern about the changes brought about by the Redditch New Town Development.

Despite the onslaught of ill health, his love of the countryside and written word remained. In letters hand written to me with failing eye-sight during 2004 the year before he died, he recalls many family events, and refers with fondness to books given to him by our father's sister Florence and half-sister Alice. As Katrina writes above, the books covered his favourite authors, Shakespeare, Dickens, the Bible and many more, all beautifully illustrated together with his notes. His memory remained sharp and the letters (which I still have) were a pleasure to read. Roy died in hospital in Bromsgrove 31st January 2005, at the age of 83.

Tina Emily Webb-Moore
07.09.2013

Tina E Webb-Moore

Tina E Webb-Moore was born **Tina Emily Webb** of Redditch, Worcestershire in the UK's West Midlands, shortly before WWII where she spent most of her formative years. She is a graduate of Redditch College, now part of North East Worcestershire College, where she majored in business and education. She was an active member of St George's Church, Redditch where she met Michael Kidger whom she later married on 26th November 1960. After their marriage Michael worked at Rank Taylor Hobson in Leicester and Tina was personal assistant to Prof. of Mathematics R. L. Goodstein at Leicester University. When Michael left Rank Taylor Hobson in Leicester to pursue his PhD and subsequent academic career at Imperial College, London in 1963 Tina supported him allowing him complete freedom to successfully develop his personally satisfying and rewarding career. Together they raised two children, David and Julia. During this time they moved from Leicester to the suburbs of London and then to East Sussex.

In 1982, Tina and Michael undertook the development and marketing of the first fully functional line of UK developed optical design software under the brand name of SIGMA, and the company name 'Kidger Optics Ltd'. With Tina as Managing Director, development of the very successful SIGMA software continued through various upgrades and versions to the final 1998 release of SIGMA 2100. Together they travelled to the United States, where they exhibited the SIGMA software at meetings of The Society of Photo-Optical Instrumentation Engineers (SPIE).

Not long after the release of SIGMA 2100 Michael died unexpectedly while on a teaching trip to Australia. Following Michael's death, Tina continued to manage Kidger Optics as a design consultancy rather than a software developer. She collected together Michael's many course notes and with the invaluable help of colleagues, two volumes of Michael's work were published posthumously, "Fundamental Optical Design" (2001) and "Intermediate Optical Design" (2004).

Tina has said that she owes her appreciation and love of nature to her father, Thomas Sydney Webb, with whom she took many walks in the Worcestershire countryside. Consequently, she has been very strongly committed, through much arduous, artistic and loving work, to designing and tending the gardens of the different homes where she has lived – she is a true English gardener.

Tina was remarried in 2002 to Emery L. Moore, PhD, an engineer/physicist and former President of SPIE. Together, they split their time between the UK and USA.

In 2011, Tina undertook the task of organizing and compiling her brother Roy's writings in a coherent manner for publication. The results of her undertaking are reflected in the volume presented here. It is hoped that many members of the larger UK community will find themselves experiencing a sympathetic journey wandering about the twentieth century West Midlands with Roy Webb.

Emery L Moore
5 September 2013

Foreword

OUR FAMILY, the Webbs of Feckenham, Studley and Redditch: Because the Webbs have been so numerous within the counties of Warwickshire and Worcestershire, and because I do not currently have at my disposal an all-encompassing Webb family tree, I am interested in outlining for the reader the particular branch of the Webb family that has a direct line with my brother Roy and myself. It is my hope that others, both Webbs and those living in or knowledgeable of the communities and people who influenced the Webbs, might enjoy these contents and possibly pass on their knowledge of some related experiences.

As far as I have traced our Webb family line to date, it lies firstly (c. 1700) in the heart of Feckenham, later in Studley and later still in Redditch. My Great Great Grandfather John Webb, was born in 1786. He lived in the Feckenham Mill (Scouring Mill) in Feckenham in the 1820s, until his death in 1849. John is buried in the churchyard of St John The Baptist, Feckenham. Earlier records, currently under review, continue John's family link within Feckenham. John and his wife had eight children, all of whom were baptized at St John The Baptist Church, Feckenham.

My Great Grandfather, Edmund Webb, born in Feckenham in 1822, is listed as a needle manufacturer, and later as owner of a grocery and drapery shop. He lived firstly in Feckenham and then in Studley where he died. Edmund and his wife had seven children most of whom after their death were buried in St Mary's Churchyard in Studley.

Thomas, my Grandfather, was born in Feckenham in 1853. He is listed at the age of 28 as a Foreman in the Needle Pointing department in the local needle manufacturing factory. Later records show that he lived at The Slough in Studley. He is buried in the churchyard of St Peter's Church, Coughton.

Thomas Sydney, my Father, was born in Studley in 1887. He married my Mother at St Peter's Church, Coughton. He worked for most of his life in an administrative position at the Austin Motor Works, Longbridge, Birmingham and they lived in Redditch. He died in 1965. My *brother scattered his ashes in the woodlands in Studley.

It is my firm belief that the Webb family maintains a continuing presence as part of the soul of the communities of Feckenham, Studley and Redditch and their surrounds. These communities are constantly present in my mind and thoughts and will remain so for always.

Tina E Webb-Moore, Malvern, Worcestershire.

(Ref Chapter 1, The Two Journeys to The Slough, Studley)

Acknowledgements

EVERY effort has been made to thank everyone who has in some way contributed to this book and to acknowledge their copyright. However, special thanks are given to Robin Whittaker, Chairman of Worcester Historical Society, who introduced me to my publishers History Into Print of Studley, and to Alan and Alistair Brewin and their staff for their considerable assistance in producing the book.

I would also like to thank Charlotte Wood and her colleagues of Redditch Borough Council who were so helpful and gave their permission to include the conservation and green belt information for Redditch.

Much thanks is due to Rob Orland who was so generous with his support in giving me permission to use text and photographs from his Coventry Cathedral website. Additionally, my thanks to Brian Skeys who generously gave his time in searching out photographs from his private collection and for also taking photographs for particular parts of the book.

Thank you to Ed Vozenilek whose photograph of the North American Grey squirrel (with the white tail) was perfect for the "Fate of Red Squirrels" story and to Patricia Heming great granddaughter of Grandmother Gazey who kindly gave permission to publish her letter and who was so helpful in providing information and photographs for the Addendum about Ellen Elizabeth Gazey.

I owe considerable thanks to Andrew Waters, Communications Officer for RSPB in the Midlands and his colleagues. From the outset of putting this book together Andy gave his advice and support, supplying current information about RSPB activities and also beautiful photographs.

I would like to thank Keith Watkins for his photographs of St Leonard's Church, Beoley, also his wife Sue.

Thanks are also due to Helen Clarke, News Editor of the Redditch and Alcester Advertiser for her permission to use my brother's letters sent to the Redditch Indicator and Redditch Advertiser over the years.

Most of all, my thanks are due to my brother's daughter, Katrina Webb, who gave permission for me to publish her father's work posthumously.

Before Roy's death in January 2005, Katrina asked her father what he would like her to do with all his writings. His answer was simply, "It's up to you."

About five years later Katrina discussed with me what should be done with the writings and I agreed to make an attempt to put the material together in a way which would be of interest to both local and wider communities of Worcestershire and Warwickshire and to those interested in lifestyle events in a small UK town throughout the 20th century and earlier. I agreed to organize and present my brother's writings in a coherent manner which would provide a testimony of his observations of the times and places he experienced. Katrina spent a great deal of time searching through her father's papers and family photographs, typing up some of the papers, and putting together other information that she thought might be of help. She passed the documents on to me as she found them, together with family photographs. The organization of this material has taken place over a period of two years during which time Katrina has continued to help wherever possible.

Finally I would like to thank my husband Emery, who helped me in so very many ways in producing this book, for his support, encouragement and advice during the many discussions we shared about my brother's writing.

Tina Emily Webb-Moore

Introduction

*Our parents Sydney Webb with his wife
Annie and Roy 1922.*

THE challenge in putting my brother's poems, essays and letters into a book, was to encourage you the reader to want to read his work, and to make all of what he wrote relevant and interesting for today and to all ages, not just in the town of Redditch and the areas of Worcestershire and Warwickshire. These events or something like them could have happened anywhere, at any time and are still happening in other towns and countries now.

I have grouped the writings under ten chapter headings including an Epilogue. The first chapter includes a detailed description of a local walk, now long since gone. The second chapter includes details of Roy's life as a boy in Beoley Road, the people who lived there, the events that took place. You can take a visit to the movies, the circus or even try spotting an air ship.

Chapter three is entirely devoted to Roy's poem about his first love, and contrasts sharply with chapter four which covers the outbreak of World War II and the results of war, then finally peace, marriage and the birth of his daughter.

Chapter five discusses several town issues of Redditch, which perturbed or moved my brother from tree planting, to land values, market issues, nurses and the Alexandra Hospital.

Chapter six is a rather large chapter so is split into three sections: "People", "Places" and "Events". The first section "People" introduces several local people and notable events in their lives and includes a poetic comment on the death of Diana, Princess of Wales. In "Places" we are taken on a history lesson around Warwickshire and Worcestershire, with its beautiful buildings and areas as Roy experienced them at the time. The final section on "Events" is a history lesson of a different kind, from the "Black Dog of Arden" to a meeting of the Redditch Poetry Circle, and even a local murder in the early 1900s.

Chapter seven covers the Liturgy of Anglican Churches, followed by a discussion of some of our English terms of expression, and then finally the delightful letter about the Pocket Oxford Dictionary.

Chapter eight will give those of you with a particular love of birds some delightful readings and poetry together with exceptional bird photographs from members of the Royal Society for the Protection of Birds (RSPB). Throughout the book you will see references at the bottom of the page to "Give Nature a Home" or "State of Nature". "Give Nature a Home" is an RSPB initiated project to encourage citizens to help create habitat conducive to nature's husbandry. "State of Nature" refers to a report compiled by a partnership between 25 organizations, including RSPB, which is a health check of nature in the UK and its Overseas Territories. Extensive information on each of these efforts has been included in the Appendices for your reference.

Chapter nine covers "Conservation" including, poems and essays about flowers, birds and trees. You will find an appendices reference with specific writings, taking you to detailed conservation information on the subject of the writing.

INTRODUCTION

Chapter ten is the Epilogue – a manuscript synopsis.

Finally I have put together an addendum and several appendices for the reader, which will give you information about many aspects of the book that you may like to explore further. This book is about my brother's journey through life, but from the beginning I have hoped to inspire you the reader to possibly take a similar journey, that is one of discovery for you in your world, which may provide you with lasting memories of pleasant and comparable experiences. I wish you as much happiness and fulfillment from your exploration and conservation of nature that I and my brother experienced through the eyes of my father and the love of nature that he gave to us.

Some of my brother's work has been edited, but otherwise it is as he recorded at the time.

Tina Emily Webb-Moore

Chapter 1

Roy Webb And Two Journeys

The Two Journeys

Roy with our mother and sisters
Doreen and Mary 1928.

WHEN I was young I lived with my parents and sisters in the small town of Redditch, Worcestershire about three miles from my father's boyhood home, a cottage in The Slough in the village of Sambourne in Studley. The home was near to an extensive wood of mixed deciduous trees where badgers and foxes had their setts and dens. Nightingales filled the calm spring evenings with their joyous bubbling rhapsodies. Next door to the family home was a second cottage where my father's half-brother George lived with his wife Beatrice. There was a meadow behind the cottage leading to a spinney with a shallow stream. I had happy memories of this quiet place where we picked primroses in April.

Bluebells in Malvern Worcestershire © T Kidger.

In May, the bluebells spread a shimmering carpet beneath the trees.

When autumn came with its abundant spoils, there were clusters of sun-browned hazelnuts to be gathered from the spinney. The hedges were laden with glistening blackberries, the sweetest of which grew near the stream. My uncle's long garden yielded baskets full of purple damsons with juicy golden flesh, from a group of tangled old trees, whose leaves tied the heavy bunches of fruit, dusted gently with bloom, as though by a fairy's hand.

The magic of this peaceful corner of rural Warwickshire had entered my eager young soul and I made up my mind that I would walk there one weekend and renew my acquaintance with its charms. After a short period of parental opposition, it was agreed that I could make the journey on condition that I asked another boy to accompany me. I persuaded one of my school friends to do so, but when I called for him on the appointed day his mother would not let him go. Undeterred, I set off alone on a sunny June morning in the year 1928. My way lay along a sunken narrow lane with no footpath and a steep clay bank on my left. This was soon followed by tall hedgerows on either side – mainly hawthorn interlaced with briars and brambles, with sturdy oaks and tufted elms at frequent intervals. Not quite seven years of age, I was short of stature and unable to see many of the fields, and much of my walk was like a progress along a green tunnel with sunbeams slanting down on to the dusty road. Countless birds fluttered in and out of the bushes urgently feeding their nestlings, concealed in these twiggy retreats. The roadside banks were tall with cocksfoot grass (*Dactylisglomerita*), wild parsley, buttercups and red clover. The May blossom had withered and fallen, having played its part in the colourful pageant, and now the stage was held by the fragile dog-rose (*Rosa canina*), the honeysuckle branches, and the heavy-scented flowers of the elderberry.

Half-way to Studley, I passed Greenland's farm drowsing in the summer warmth. The smell of new mown hay reached me from one of the lower fields. A plump guinea fowl, perched high on the ridge of the barn betrayed my presence with its shrill persistent call, which continued until I had walked some distance from the farm.

At eleven o'clock I arrived at the corner of Green Lane, on the northern edge of Studley. Pigeons were cooing on the warm roof tiles of a farmhouse. In the garden a small dog of doubtful pedigree barked with vigour, and made a determined dash down the path, this alarmed me, but he stopped at the gate and ceased to bark, subjecting me instead to a close canine scrutiny.

A few yards along Green Lane a narrow strip of turf studded with daisies was crossed by a short footpath which led to a stile. Sitting upon the stile with an air of indolent contentment was a one-legged man. Unshaven and collarless, he had thin black hair, a sharp face and an alert eye in which I thought I detected the ghost of a twinkle. He fixed me with a keen look, while scratching his chest through his open shirt.

"Ha! Ha!" cried the one-legged man, "where have you come from?"

"From Redditch," said I.

"Bless my soul! That's a fair walk for a youngster like you and what might your name be my lad?" I told him that my name was Webb, upon receipt of which intelligence he uttered an exclamation of surprise, and informed me that his name also was Webb. "Now ain't that a most remarkable thing?" said he, to which I agreed. At this moment, a tousle-haired youth of about 18 came from a cottage on the other side of the lane. "You see him?" said my one-legged friend, "His name is Webb too!" This seemed to me somewhat improbable, but I did not dispute the fact, since the newcomer nodded his head and smiled in agreement, when the question was put to him. Another young man then appeared upon the scene and earnestly laid claim to the same surname. Too polite to contradict the assembled company, but unconvinced by their assertions of our patronymic (*paternal family name*) identity, I took my leave of them.

I passed beneath a railway bridge by an orchard of tall pear trees, crossed a hayfield and finally reached my uncle's gate shortly before noon. I can see that friendly little gate now, painted green it hung slightly awry, and needed a gentle lift to open it. I knocked upon the door, which was opened by my uncle. Normally a man of placid disposition, his eyes widened with surprise when he looked down upon his small and unexpected visitor. "How did you get here?" he asked.

"I walked, uncle."

"Come in, come in and sit down," said he with a laugh, "you must be tired." He and his wife made me most welcome, enquired after my family, and regaled me with a glass of cold milk and a large slice of home-made cake. Before leaving I walked down the field to the spinney to pick some foxgloves, and proudly gave them to my aunt. I walked home by the same route but remember nothing of the journey.

I later established the true identity of the one-legged man. His name was Gus Dyer, and in the winter months he was a tireless follower of the local hunt. Gus knew the area and he invariably kept up with the riders and hounds as they pursued a fox, and was a popular character with the members of the hunt.

In the years that followed, my father and I made many pleasant trips to Studley, sometimes on our pedal cycles, and later by public transport.

My last visit had a solemn purpose and took place when I was 43. My father had died suddenly at the age of 77, and was cremated in Birmingham. It was decided at a family conference that his ashes should be scattered in his beloved spinney. I readily assented to perform this task.

The first Saturday in April found me seated on a bus, holding a grey canister which contained the mortal remains of my father. In this way he made his last journey home. It was a warm day with a brassy sun staring down from a blue and white sky, like a huge china plate.

The narrow lane of my childhood pilgrimage had been widened, and carried a heavy flow of traffic. Trees and hedgerows had gone, grass verges were now concrete pavements. In the intervening years all of Greenland's farm land had been covered with houses and factories. The farmhouse had disappeared. One broken apple tree stood forlorn in a neglected patch which had been the farm orchard. The hayfield opposite my uncle's home had also been built upon. Neat red houses with tidy gardens and trim lawns covered the former enclosure of succulent grasses and rich clover, haunted by small moths and butterflies, and redolent of summer dreams. The damson trees were succumbing to age and decay. "We never get any damsons now," said my aunt.

Only the spinney was unchanged, constant in its beauty and its magic and I felt the rightness of what I was about to do. The little stream still wound between the hazel bushes and the alder trees. A male blackbird flew off clamorously, and a bright-eyed robin came to investigate my arrival, hopping from bush to bush in a circle around me. The primroses, violets and anemones were in flower, as though patiently waiting for us and ready to play their part in this act of reunion.

First leaves of spring 2011 © E Moore.

I scattered my father's ashes beneath the hazel trees, some fell among the primroses and the new bluebell shoots, some drifted gently with the wind into the quiet water, to be borne slowly away to the river and on to the eternal sea. My heart was at peace within me as I left the spinney and returned to the noisy road. I had kept faith with my father he would have desired no other resting place.

20 June 1966

Conservation (Ref Apps E and F) state of nature

Chapter 2

How It Was

1920s & 1930s

Recollections of life in Beoley Road, Redditch in the 1920s

Brian's Garden in Hanley Swan, Worcestershire © B Skeys.

Horses

It was a dry and windy day in March, in the small industrial town of Redditch in the Midlands. Scraps of paper fluttered along the pavements and clouds of grit and dust rose from the gutters. In Beoley Road, thin shafts of pale sunlight fell between the houses and lit up the road, which descended with varying degrees of steepness from the church at the top of the hill, to the muddy brook where the houses ended half a mile below. Beyond lay a quiet countryside of rough pastures and overgrown hedges.

Half-way down Beoley Road, on the left-hand side, a narrow entry gave access to a backyard which was shared by four houses. The mouth of the entry was raised above the pavement by a single step, upon which stood a thin, fair-haired boy about eight years old. His pale face had freckles and his grey eyes had an abstracted air which belied the acuteness of his observation as he looked up and down the road. Though withdrawn and dreamy, he was thoroughly aware of what was happening.

Roy, 7 years old.

He watched two sparrows quarrelling over a stale crust in a nearby garden and saw the stealthy approach of a battle-scarred cat, which brought a speedy end to avian hostilities and the precipitate flight of the protesting birds.

The boy's main interest, however, was in the horses which regularly worked in the street. The horses, patient plodding creatures were an essential part of the daily scene at this time, when motor vehicles were uncommon.

There was the old white mare which drew the milk cart, freshly painted in yellow and green, and bearing in elegant black letters the legend

"A. Day, Proctors Barn Farm, Beoley."

The cart carried two large churns, from which the farmer's delivery pail was replenished from time to time. Mr Day was unfailingly punctual in his milk round. Winter and summer for many years his cart would arrive alongside the entry at eight o'clock in the morning. The mare would stop without his bidding and the farmer with a firm deliberate tread, would carry his pail up the entry to serve his customers in the yard. The boy's Mother produced a white quart jug, into which the milk was carefully dispensed from two measures which hung, each by a small hook, from a rim inside the pail. The boy, fascinated, would watch this daily ritual, with the steady movements of the farmer's large red hands, his wrists protected in the cold weather by grey woollen mittens, leaving his fingers free for their painstaking work.

The coal cart, stacked high with hundredweight sacks, was pulled by a chestnut gelding. This long-suffering animal was enlivened at frequent intervals by sharp flicks of the whip, together with a stream of equally cutting remarks from the driver, these comments, delivered in a rough penetrating voice, were derogatory of the horse's appearance, intelligence, industry and ancestry.

The heavy railway wagon was the earthly burden of a huge black carthorse called Prince, with broad glistening flanks, thick legs and massive hooves – a giant of a horse, the epitome of equine strength. But one morning Prince suddenly dropped dead in the shafts and much difficulty was experienced in freeing the harness and removing the carcass from the road.

The butcher, phlegmatic, rubicund and very fat, sat in a smart gig which was drawn by a willing and vigorous pony, whose high-stepping hooves struck sparks from the hard road. The boy felt sorry to see this small pony pulling such a heavy and inert mass of human flesh, but the fine-fettled pony was equal to the task which indeed he appeared to enjoy and the gig always went up the road at a spanking pace, which none of the other horses could hope to equal.

There was a small covered wagon of unusual appearance, which made regular journeys from Beoley Paper Mill to the railway station. This was a cart with a semi-circular canvas hood, the purpose of which was to protect from the elements its precious load – a single gigantic roll of white paper. The custodian of this equipage was old, cloth-capped and walrus-moustached, his leisurely disposition was shared by his four-footed partner, to whom the name Pegasus had been ironically bestowed. They proceeded up the hill, slowly but with considerable dignity.

Finally, there was a "moon-faced" farmer of melancholy aspect who wore a floppy grey felt hat and who delivered milk by horse and cart from his farm at *Morton Bagot. The farm was some distance away, along the green winding lanes, where the tiny church, with lambs nibbling beneath its ancient walls, was adjacent to his farmyard, and long stemmed violets grew under the willows…

The Art Class

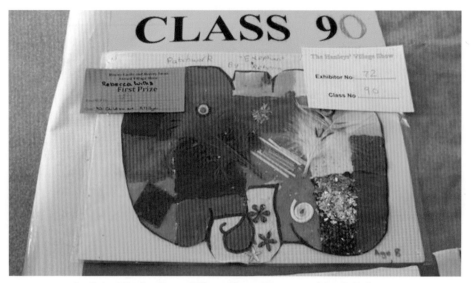

1st Prize Hanley Swan Village Show, Worcestershire © Rebecca.

There was a low-roofed cottage near to the Church of England school which the boy attended where a widow lived. Her kitchen window displayed glass jars containing home-made sweets and toffee, which she sold in pennyworths to the local children. The front garden to the cottage was a colourful, if unruly mass of flowers, and trained around the cottage door was a yellow jasmine in full flower.

It was Tuesday, when the first lesson in the afternoon at school was drawing, a subject which the boy enjoyed. He had some artistic ability, and enjoyed creating a picture. This day the pupils had been asked by their teacher to bring a flower to draw.

Attracted by the small golden blossoms of the jasmine, he timidly approached the door and knocked gently upon it. The old lady appeared, a ragged shawl hanging upon her bent shoulders, leaning heavily on a black stick. She eyed him sharply and asked him what he wanted. "Please… may I have a piece of your jasmine to draw in school?" "No you can't" was the curt reply. "I don't grow my jasmine for other folk." The boy went away feeling puzzled and disappointed. Nevertheless, he was shocked and sorry when some months later the old lady was forcibly carried from her home and taken to hospital because she was no longer capable of caring for herself. Like a plant uprooted, she soon withered away and died within a few weeks.

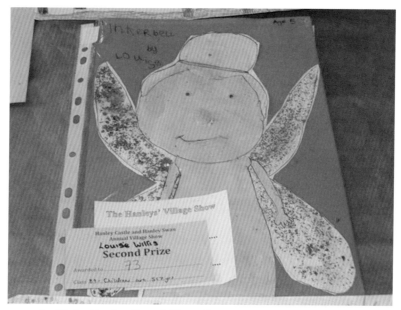

2nd Prize Hanley Swan Village Show, Worcestershire © Louise.

Thirty Years Later

Thirty years later, after many wanderings, the boy returned to his native town. The row of cottages where the old lady lived had given way to a three-storey block of flats, and there were no horses to be seen in the street, which now carried an unceasing flow of motor-cars. Beoley Paper Mill, he later discovered was derelict and Proctors Barn Farm had been demolished by the Local Authority, the site was overgrown with rank grass and a solitary rose bush, half choked with bindweed, was the only evidence that this had been the garden of a farmhouse. A visit to Morton Bagot revealed that the lane had been widened and drainage works installed, and he looked in vain for the delicate long-stemmed violets.

14th June 1966

* The Church of the Holy Trinity, Morton Bagot, dates from the 13th Century, and still retains many ancient features.

*(Ref App D)

Author's Note:

My brother writes in the third person here recalling his personal memories. It is a movie in miniature of two separate moments in time. He never did leave Redditch.

WORKING HORSES IN THE 1920s

In this mechanized age with its frantic rush it is pleasant to recall a time when working horses and ponies were often seen on the streets and in the fields, and cars and tractors were few. This period was the twenty years before 1939 when life was slower, quieter and perhaps more interesting.

There were different horses for different jobs, of course. Heavy Shires (as big as elephants) pulled the plough or drew the farm carts and harvest wagons. The numerous milkmen used smaller horses in the shafts of their floats, while Mr. Bowen of Battens Farm, Icknield Street, would turn out with a smart pony and trap.

Godfrey Bomford of Marlfield Farm kept his big horses in the old stable which is now known to Church Hill residents as "Marlfield Barn". Charlie Griffin (aged 15) from Ipsley Mill Cottages did a milk round in Redditch every morning before school.

After the war, the Railway Goods Department was motorized and the horses were sold by auction at Barnt Green market. Some of the railway men wept at parting from their friends and workmates.

These jottings will interest older residents of Redditch like myself and may give newcomers a faint picture of the town as it was.

14th March 1991

MOVIES – PALACE THEATRE

The Palace Theatre (opened in 1913). In the 1920s and 1930s, it was a cinema which showed black and white silent movies – admission 2d (= *2 pennies*) in the "Pit" and 6d (= *6 pennies*) in the balcony. Matinees were held on Wednesday and Saturday with two separate houses in the evenings.

In the "Well of the Pit" below the screen, a small live orchestra supplied background music. Piano, fiddle and drum produced realistic sound effects – e.g. galloping horses, rushing trains and gentle "sloppy" stuff for the romantic interludes. Sometimes I would go to a Saturday afternoon show. I especially remember "The Kid" (1921) (Charlie Chaplin and Jackie Coogan), "Song of Songs" (1933) (Marlene Dietrich and Brian Aherne), "The Laughing Man" (1928) (Conrad Veidt) and "Tugboat Annie" (1933) (Wallace Beery and Marie Dresler).

"The Laughing Man" is Victor Hugo's classic story of England in the time of Queen Anne. I still have a copy of the book published by the Readers Library at 6d which contains photographic stills from the old film.

The first talkie was with Al Jolson "The Jazz Singer" (1927).

The Redditch Advertiser 21st March 1990

Palace Theatre (Ref App G)

Author's Note:

On 7th September 2013, the Palace Theatre put on a show celebrating 100 years of the Palace Theatre, Redditch, 1913 – 2013, with a "Centenary Celebration Show" featuring the local operatic societies from Redditch, Astwood Bank and Studley, also the Alcester Musical Theatre Company "The Harlequins". The event was hosted by Don Maclean.

GRAHAM COURT, HIS DOG AND A BADGER
Beoley Road, Redditch. Part of a letter from Roy to an unknown friend

… cruel to animals, he gloried especially in the killing of foxes.

One day in the 1930s Graham went to Marlfield Farm and obtained permission from the farmer Godfrey Bomford to dig a badger from its sett (*badger's den*) in the field opposite the farmhouse. He put his terrier dog "Tiger" into the hole to drive the badger out. Tiger went in but did not come out. He was fighting for his life against the badger, who was fiercely defending his home.

After digging all night, Graham unearthed the badger which he then killed, and rescued Tiger more dead than alive. The next morning he carried Tiger to the Vet's surgery who said, "There is nothing we can do for this dog. He is dying, and you should be prosecuted for cruelty to animals."

Tiger did not die. Graham nursed and fed him until his wounds were healed. The dog never went hunting again but spent most of his time in the back yard. Nevertheless, I liked Graham, he was an unforgettable character.

Kind regards to yourself and your wife.

Undated

Author's Note:

Although I did not know Graham Court, I spent many happy hours playing with his son also called Graham who lived nearby. A favourite activity would be to go fishing in the brook which my brother refers to as part of the River Arrow, later diverted by the New Town Development. There with our fishing nets we would catch small fish and put them in a jam-jar of water, where unfortunately they did not live long. Tiger who nearly lost his life, was a small black dog with long hair and would sit quite comfortably guarding the door to his home.

ABOUT SID GREEN, BARBER
Beoley Road, Redditch

… there was a barber's shop on this site 70 years ago. The Proprietor, Sid Green, was a short, fat man, a bachelor and a well- known character in Beoley Road, very fussy and methodical, he took great pride in his waxed moustaches.

He was kind to the boys – his charge for a boy's haircut was 4d. Each boy was given a comic to read while waiting and a few sweets in a triangular paper bag on leaving the shop.

At 65 Sid retired to Cheltenham, where he became very lonely and longed for his friends in Redditch. He said at the time, "I watered the streets of Cheltenham with my tears." So he returned to Beoley Road, hired a couple of rooms in a house near the Post Office and went back to work with his scissors and hand clippers (he refused to use electric clippers when they were introduced).

He died of a sudden heart attack when he got up one night to put a shilling in the electric meter.

Undated

CIRCUS HAS COME TO TOWN: 1930s
Elephants on Parade

Sixty years ago the monotony of the summer holidays from school would be enlivened by the annual visit of Pat Collins Fun Fair to Beoley Road Recreation Ground. For a few days the normally quiet field would be all noise, lights and novel attractions to coax the pennies from your pocket.

There were also Circus visits, when one would lie in bed at night in Beoley Road and hear the lions' roar, and be glad they were safely locked up. One morning as a young man I visited the "Wagon and Horses", public house in Beoley Road, and refreshed myself with two or three pints of cider. On leaving the pub, the very first things that I saw were three elephants walking sedately down the road in single file, which made me wonder about the strength of the cider I had just consumed. It was no hallucination of course, the "Circus had come to Town".

The Redditch Advertiser 8th March 1992

Author's Note:
The UK government recently announced that a ban prohibiting the use of wild animals in circuses in Britain would come into effect in 2015.

CATCHING A PIKE
A November day in the 1930s

Northern Pike (known as pike in Britain). Courtesy U.S. Fish and Wildlife Service

About a mile from a small industrial town (*Redditch*) in the Midlands there is a quiet pond, which at one time supplied the water power for an adjacent Needle Mill. Several acres in extent, the pond is almost completely divided by a narrow tongue of land, which terminates a few yards from its eastern bank. This green causeway, overgrown and difficult of access, provides a secluded nesting site for a pair of swans, who annually rear their brood in a large nest. The nest is sheltered by one of the many *alder trees, whose twiggy branches are reflected in the glassy pool below, except where broken by the floating leaves of water-lilies. The shores are thick with rushes, and the banks with wild rose bushes, which flaunt their fragile flowers – some pink, some white – in the hot days of June.

In the long, calm days before the last war, the pond was the mecca of all the youthful anglers in the district and known locally as the "Broad Waters", its muddy depths held some fine roach, perch and pike. But the freedom of this place was denied to us: the fishing was strictly private, and the banks were patrolled by two stern guards: the Water Bailiff, who lived in a nearby cottage, and the farmer, whose land adjoined the pond.

The water bailiff was a quick, rosy-faced little man, whose otherwise placid existence was enlivened by alarms and excursions in pursuit of boyish intruders upon his watery domain.

The grey-whiskered farmer was burly and grim; seventy winters had ploughed deep furrows upon his brow, but he was still strong and active, and his heavy build belied his stealthy tread. Wearing a rough suit of antique cut, a battered felt hat and a stiff stand-up collar, he would appear silently from the misty fields to startle many an unsuspecting young fisherman, and to frustrate his hopes with the curt advice to "be off, before I throw you and your rods into the water."

Fishing here, therefore, instead of being a peaceful, leisurely occupation, was a battle of wits, and took the form of lightning forays, with a wary eye to the right in the direction of the water bailiff's cottage and another to the left against the unwelcome arrival of the irascible farmer. In these expeditions, organisation and speed were essential, and constant vigilance was the watchword. It was a cold, dull morning in November when I saw this technique practiced to perfection.

A heavy frost had blackened much of the aquatic vegetation, and the alder branches were encrusted with grime. The only noise was the plaintive song of a robin in a hawthorn bush near the sluice-gates. The surface of the pond was like a steel mirror, and the pike was hungry.

Four youths appeared from the narrow path which runs behind a high privet hedge from the pool to the public highway. They carried no fishing rods, only a thin cord, about forty yards in length. Fastened to this was a steel trace, which bore a large hook. The hook was baited on the spot with a lively minnow, whereupon the line was vigorously cast into the pond, and drawn quickly through the water, the minnow flashing silver, the deadly hook concealed in its back. Almost immediately, there was a strong flurry a few feet away, a swift, aggressive approach as the pike hurled itself upon the hapless minnow, and a thrashing turmoil when the hook struck deep into its vicious jaw. The line was pulled in without a pause and lifted over the bank, and a well-marked pike of six or seven pounds lay gasping and snapping in the frosty grass. A pair of rough, red hands disgorged the hook, the line was retrieved, and the pike was killed and borne away in triumph.

The pond returned to its accustomed stillness; and the water bailiff, at breakfast in his warm kitchen, helped himself to another slice of buttered toast, unaware of this daring raid. The pike would have provided a sumptuous meal for a poor family.

Roy Webb c 1946

*Alder (Ref App A) Conservation (Ref Apps E and F) state of nature

WATERY LANE – REDDITCH 1930s

Older residents of Redditch will recall the original Watery Lane, a sunken narrow lane, lined with hawthorn bushes and haunted by yellow hammers that led from the Studley Road to Ipsley Mill. A pleasant spot to linger was on the first bridge which crossed the River Arrow in its old channel before it was "re-aligned".

The river was shaded by many indigenous brook *Alders. Its banks were bright with balsam flowers whose seed pods exploded at a touch. To the right of the bridge the water flowed smoothly down the spill-way into a pool below, where it divided to embrace a small green island.

One spring day when the brook was dappled with sunlight a small bird had woven its nest on the low branch of an alder at a point which was no more than a foot above the water level. A precarious perch, I thought, for the fledglings.

This was a delightful place to stand and stare or lean against the parapet of the bridge and listen to the water where it rippled over its pebbles in the shallows, before the route of the river was changed by the Redditch Development Corporation.

25th July 1991

Alders (Ref App A) Conservation (Ref App E) (Ref App F) state of nature

SPOTTING THE AIRSHIP in 1932
(Reply to letter from Mr. Sly)

On Sunday July 3 1932 when the German *Airship passed over Redditch, my father and I saw it from Beoley Road recreation ground at about noon, having just left St George's Church.

It was rumoured that she was taking photographs for use in wartime.

Mr. Sly may be confusing the Graf Zeppelin with its British counterpart R101 which crashed on a hill in Northern France.

The Redditch Advertiser – 28th May 1992

Airship (Ref App G)

THROWING STONES AT GRANDMOTHER GAZEY'S DUCKS (ELLEN ELIZABETH GAZEY)

*Ellen Elizabeth Gazey with grandson Gerald,
in front of 253 Beoley Road circa 1930/31.*

In the years before the Second World War a family that lived at 253 Beoley Road, Redditch had a small holding. This small farm (Gazey Fields) comprising two rough fields of about an acre, lay in an angle of the *River Arrow, between the bridge that crossed The Brook (River Arrow), at the bottom of Beoley Road, and the Beoley Mill Cottages about a mile further on.

This brambly piece of land supported an interesting menagerie of cocks and hens, turkeys, pigs, two or three cows and a few ducks on the brook.

**Grandmother Gazey the old lady who did most of the work on the farm was a wizened little woman, with a weather-beaten face like a wrinkled walnut.

One day, when I was standing with other boys on the bridge she shouted angrily:

"I know who you are and you have been throwing stones at my ducks and driving them down the river. I know your fathers and I'll tell them when I see them."

I had never seen any boys throwing stones at the ducks and it certainly wasn't me. The old bridge has gone, so have the animals and ducks, and Mrs Gazey has been "At Rest" these many years.

Addendum

*River Arrow "Wading through the waters of the brook", page 101. Ordnance Survey Map 1887, page 104

**Grandmother Gazey, Ellen Elizabeth Gazey (Ref)

LETTER FROM THE GREAT GRANDDAUGHTER OF GRANDMOTHER GAZEY
Patricia M Heming, Wales
IN REPLY TO ROY WEBB

Ellen in Gazey Fields wearing her Sunday Apron.

I read with interest a letter recently published in your paper sent in by Roy Webb. It was brought to my family's attention by friends who still live in Redditch.

Mr. Webb's letter refers to my great grandmother, *Grandmother Gazey. By reputation the old lady was certainly tough, but it was only with her grim determination that she was able to overcome the hard knocks that life bestowed on her. She was widowed at an early age and left to bring up five children. To help make ends meet she took in washing, as well as keeping her odd assortment of farm animals.

Many older Redditch people may still remember her two daughters Nell and Jinny (Jin) who looked after the poultry long after their mother's death and continued to live in the same house, 253 Beoley Road until the late 1960s.

Not only did they look after "Gazey Fields" as it was known, but with the help of one of their brothers they also looked after two allotments. One was at the back of Sillins Avenue and they kept up the family tradition of keeping pigs there until well into the 1950s. The other was in Lady Harriet's Lane and here they grew wonderful pears which they sold from the house.

As a matter of interest with the exception of Frederick William who was born in Redhill, Warwickshire, Granny Gazey's other children were born at the old **Toll House, Bordesley, another former Redditch landmark, now long since gone.

Maybe the old girl was a bit of a tartar, but certainly many a young lad chased her ducks down over "The Black Soils" which took her time she could ill afford to lose to get them back. Her family certainly remembers her with pride, even if she was a bit of a character.

As for me, I missed knowing her by just a few years. She died in 1943 at the good old age of 83.

The Redditch Advertiser 12 December 1991

Grandmother Gazey, Ellen Elizabeth Gazey (Ref Addendum)

**Toll House (Ref App G)*

POLLUTION before 1993

Roy writes:

The streets were dirty in the summer and muddy in the winter – "miry ways" were common. A plentiful source of dust came from the coal fires which most house holders had. This dust also created atmospheric pollution resulting in smog in built up areas.

The Redditch Advertiser 11th November 1991

The Author writes:

Industrial areas with smoke pouring from chimneys from factories and private homes which burnt solid fuel, resulted in poor air conditions. It was particularly bad when there was a fog which resulted in a smoke filled atmosphere, through which you could not see far, and which was bad for your health.

The Clean Air Act (1993) brought a tremendous improvement in industrial cities like Birmingham and throughout the country.

SPARROW CATCHING in the early 1900s

A hundred years ago (according to my father) village lads practiced the art of *bat fowling, that is a group of them would go out after dark carrying nets on poles with which to trap sparrows roosting on the ivy clad walls of old houses.

The birds were taken home, roasted over the fire on toasting forks and eaten.

The Redditch Advertiser 19th November 1992

House Sparrow, Tree Sparrow RSPB Breeding decline long-term BDp2**Red status** *(Ref App F)*

**Bat-fowling, was the practice of catching birds at night by blinding them with a light and then hitting or netting them. (Ref App G)*

MR BAINES, BILL POSTER.... Old Advertisements

Mr Wilkins' letter "Do you remember?" revived a few memories for me. He mentioned Baines the Bill Poster. Does Mr Wilkins remember some of the huge posters displayed on the hoardings around the town?

- "The Bisto Kids" "Ah! Bisto" – as their nostrils picked up its appetizing smell.

- "Palethorpes Sausages" – a pig harnessed to a plate laden with sausages – drawing his own conclusion.

- "McDougall's Self-Raising Flour" – a baby on its back, kicking a cake into the air.

- "A little Bovril keeps the Doctor away" – a bull calf rushing at a doctor as he approaches a farmhouse door.

- "M & B Deer's Leap" – the massive and famous enameled sign that hung on the wall of the Cricketer's Arms (public house) for many years.

The Redditch Advertiser 26th December 1991

Author's Note:
Those who are interested might like to buy a copy of "The History of Bovril Advertising" compiled by Peter Hadley for Bovril Ltd. This book is filled with old adverts for Bovril, with a good dialogue for each section, for example "Bovril and the Trade", "Sporting Bovril" and so on. The author has a 1973 copy, but copies are still available from Amazon. Bovril (Ref App. I)

CIGARETTE CARDS

The Editor, "Legion"
Royal British Legion
48 Pall Mall
London
SW1Y 5JY
10th May 1993

I read with interest the article by Neville Denson in the May issue of "Legion" on *cigarette cards.

When I was a school boy in the twenties many boys were enthusiastic collectors and would approach men smoking in the streets with, "Got any cigarette cards mister?"

We often called them "Generals" because, I believe, one of the first sets depicted the Generals of the South African War, issued by OGDENS.

Yours sincerely,

Roy Webb.

*Cigarette Cards (Ref App G)

Chapter 3

The Mutability Of Love

**"See how she leans her cheek upon her hand.
O that I were a glove upon that hand
That I might touch that cheek!"**

William Shakespeare, "Romeo and Juliet".

(23.04.1564 – 23.04.1616)

THE MUTABILITY OF LOVE

Fair Goddess stay, why haste away?
I have not glimpsed for many a day
Your dainty figure and lightsome tread,
And cheeks ablush with deepening red,

And golden hair in waving tresses
Which the playful breeze caresses,
And sparkling eyes of clearest grey
Which are so wise and yet so gay.

Why so shy, when I come nigh?
If you depart, then I shall sigh,
Then stay with me and you shall be
My mistress loved surpassingly,
And yet if you were ever near
You would wilt and fade I fear,
And lose your grace in my poor eyes,
And I no longer should you prize,
But if you went all charm you would regain,
And very soon, I should want you again.

1938

Chapter 4

War And Peace

"There will be today, there will be tomorrow, there will be always, and there was yesterday, and there was the day before..."

Leo Tolstoy, "War and Peace".

(11.09.1828 – 20.11.1910)

War

1940 THE GERMAN BLITZ OF COVENTRY

Roy Webb c1940.

The Author writes:

In 1939 my brother volunteered to join the army and as a member of the Royal Signals he was in Coventry on 14th November 1940 when the first blitz on Coventry took place.

He was on duty in the plotting room that night and had a lucky escape because his barracks were hit during the raid. He recalled to his daughter the damage to the city and cathedral, and the injured lying in the smoking ruins.

On a recent visit to the cathedral, I stood in the ruins of the old cathedral, and saw the striking and moving sight of the cross on the original altar with the prayer beneath: The Coventry Litany of Reconciliation. All of us of whatever age should know of the history of the blitz, and also learn from the reaching out to all persons of whatever religion by the building of the new cathedral. This inspiring building, with the Great West Screen of Saints and Angels, which allows you to see the ruins of the old cathedral, as you stand within the new cathedral, reminds us that all is possible, with kindness and care for our fellow man. The photographs below are by kind permission of Rob Orland, and there are further details about the history of that night of the blitz (Ref App C) www.historiccoventry.co.uk

Ruined Cathedral (St Michael's) morning of 15th November 1940.

Inside St Michael's Church (Coventry Cathedral) c 1910.

June 2006 showing new Cathedral and Cathedral Ruins.

THE LADS FROM THE HAMLETS OF ENGLAND

They were lads from the hamlets of England,
Unversed in affairs of state,
Yet in the wastes of Libya
They settled an Empire's fate.
They left their wives and sweethearts
To fight they knew not why,
They left the cool green meadows
In the burning sand to die
Their names shall be engraved on marble
But naught they'll care by then,
The meek shall inherit the earth
Six feet each for fighting men.

30th May 1943

BRAVE HEARTS – SOLDIERS AND FAMILIES

World War I – 1914-1918

In the 1920s, after the Great War (WWI), it was not uncommon to see men who had returned from the trenches who were badly disabled, hobbling about the streets, with shattered bodies or amputated limbs. The artificial limbs provided then, were very primitive by today's standards. Some of these poor fellows would stand about in the town, wearing their medal ribbons and selling bootlaces or matches.

A man like this lived nearby in Phillips Terrace (Beoley Road), Redditch, with his elderly aunt – a little old lady who wore a lace cap and walked with a stick. Alf Styler (that was his name) was badly crippled and supplemented his War Pension by doing odd jobs of painting and decorating. My Mother employed him once to do some work in the home.

Mr. James of Prospect Road, Redditch, lost both legs through frostbite on a French battlefield in World War I. His fiancée who had waited for him remained true and they married, even though he was incapable of work and needed a wheelchair to get around in. The husband of their daughter was killed on active service in the Royal Air Force in World War II.

1939-1945

Iris Cockings lived in the house opposite our home in Beoley Road. Her baby was born on the same day she was notified that her husband had been killed on active service. The War Memorial at the Redditch County High School (now Trinity High School) was the work of the Woodwork Master, Tommy Watson. He had to carve about fifteen names on that piece of English oak (all boys from the school), including that of his only son – lost at sea in about 1943.

Roy Webb undated

Military (Ref App G)

A SOLDIER'S SONG

At this golden time of year
Of fallen leaves when winter's near
I hear the tramp of marching men
Moving with measured step, an endless host
And as they march they smile and sing
Scraps of many a soldier's song.

Roy Webb
Undated

ROLLS OF HONOUR

Roll of Honour for the Royal Worcestershire Regiment 1914-1920
Deaths totalled 9,440 soldiers of all ranks including 526 officers. The total
includes about 150 who died when serving at home with the Reserve battalions
and about 200 who died of disease in Macedonia and Iraq et el. The remainder
were all killed in action or mortally wounded while serving with one or other
of the Regiments' 12 fighting battalions.

Roll of Honour for the Royal Worcestershire Regiment 1939-1947
Deaths totalled 1,013 soldiers of all ranks including 82 officers. The average
age was 26 years. Of the total men 966 were killed in action or died of wounds.
By far the greatest losses were 1944-45 when 555 lost their lives.

Details extracted from, and used with kind permission of www.roll-of-
honour.com

Roll of Honour for the Royal Warwickshire Regiment 1914-1918
Deaths totalled 11,959.

Roll of Honour for the Royal Warwickshire Regiment 1939-1945
Deaths totalled 1,115 + 152 Post WWII.

Details extracted from, and used with kind permission of www.roll-of-
honour.com

Military (Ref App G and K)

Peace
GOLD UPON THE MEADOW

Rape field, view from Malvern Hills © E Moore.

The sun shines on the road,
Creaks by a cart of straw,
My heart soars with the lark
And knows its fear no more.

The cattle go to pasture
Along the quiet lane,
And in the morning sunlight
There is an end of pain.

There is gold upon the meadow
And mist upon the hill,
The road winds on for ever
And sorrow's voice is still.

And when I reach the village
And sit down in the Inn,
The whole world will be happy
And there will be no sin.

1947

Skylark RSPB breeding decline long term BDp2**Red status**

Ref (App F) Give Nature a Home

FATHERHOOD

My brother with his wife Irene and daughter Katrina 1947.

Moments of beauty have I known,
A golden autumn morning that has spilled
The wine of sunlight on the frosty grass,
And new-born Katrina's smile has filled
My heart with surging joy

Though little in the world attained
I'd want no other if I lived again,
And having had these
I have not lived in vain

2nd October
1947

Chapter 5

Redditch Town Issues

1950s onwards

"Mr Bird, a Redditch Councillor, made a gift of his
* 'Manorial Rights' to the Council, including the rents
from the few market stalls that then comprised the Saturday Market, alongside St Stephen's Church, the originator
of the present six-day open market."

TREE PLANTING – REDDITCH 1956

I commend to the attention of the Redditch Urban District Council the circular on tree-planting issued by the Ministry of Housing and Local Government.

In Redditch on the new council estates we have a number of roads which are named after trees; pleasant sounding names which conjure up visions of arboreal beauty. But the vision is dispelled by the reality of stretches of hard pavement, unrelieved for the most part by nothing much taller than a blade of grass.

Golden Chain (Laburnum) © B Skeys.

Laburnum Close is not festooned with Golden Racemes (*Golden Chain*) in May, while the few lilacs in Lilac Close are prisoners in the policeman's garden. I have not ascertained whether the Sorbus family is represented in Rowan Road or whether Crataegus Oxyacantha (*Midland Hawthorn*) flourishes in Hawthorn Road. It would be unreasonable to expect Myrtle Avenue to be true to its exotic name, but one can hardly be other than disappointed by the treeless wastes of Willow Way and Cherry Tree Walk. Having named so many roads after trees, it seems to me that the Local Authority has a clear duty to fulfill the pledge inherent in such names. The Ministry's circular might have been written for Redditch. There are other roads in the district of course, where trees might, with much advantage, be planted.

On the score of cost (since the Minister has probably omitted to send a cheque with his circular), I suggest a "Trees for Redditch" fund be open for voluntary subscriptions, in addition to such funds as the council might be able to allocate for this purpose. A voluntary fund ought to succeed, since before very long the subscribers would be rewarded with the beauty of leaf, blossom, and berry and the graceful symmetry of twigs and branches. This would be no ephemeral beauty, since by judicious planting each succeeding season could bring its own installment of interest and delight. Having made a personal contribution, the local resident would be the more vigilant against the occasional attempt at vandalism. For a modest outlay, the attractiveness of our roads can be permanently enhanced.

"ReddichDeoFloreat" is probably bad Latin, but a good sentiment.

The Redditch Indicator 1956

Trees (Ref App E)

LAND VALUES IN REDDITCH

A comparison between 1969 and 1992

You report the case of a Winyates couple whose house sale fell through when the Ground Landlord said that the sum of £6,000 was required for the freehold of their property.

In 1969/70 a 200 acre farm at Beoley was acquired by the Development Corporation at £400 per acre. I understand that land in Redditch today is worth something like £400,000 per acre.

An acre of land will accommodate six or eight houses. At £6,000 per plot, that is some advance on £400.

The Redditch Advertiser 13th February 1992

REDDITCH COUNCILLOR
Mr H R BIRD's generous gift of Manorial Rights

From time to time one reads in the press of the sale of "Manorial Lordships", feudal titles which may carry certain rights, such as market tolls.

Before 1947 the Earl of Plymouth was Lord of the Manor of Tardebigge, which included Redditch. When the Plymouth Estate was sold, the "Lordship" passed to Mr H R Bird a member of the syndicate that acquired such estate properties not otherwise disposed of.

Mr Bird, a Redditch Councillor, made a gift of his *"Manorial Rights" to the Council, including the rents from the few market stalls that then comprised the Saturday Market, alongside St Stephen's Church, the originator of the present six-day open market. A small plaque on the wall of the Public Library acknowledges Councillor Bird's generous gift.

The Redditch Advertiser 12th June 1992

Manorial Rights and Lordships (Ref App G)

KEEP THE MARKET OFF CHURCH GREEN

With regard to the ongoing discussions about the location of Redditch Market, no one has pointed out that "Church Green" is a designated *conservation area, and so it should be the idea being to protect this green triangle from further development, and preserve it as an oasis of comparative peace in the centre of the town.

Many stall holders want the temporary move to Church Green made permanent because it is beneficial for them. The fact one side of the Green is still called the "Market Place" is irrelevant.

In my boyhood, the market was held on Saturday and consisted of less than twenty market stalls. My grandmother, Prudence Styler was one of the stall holders.

I would like to see Church Green as a small pedestrian area where one can enjoy the fountain and gardens and meet with friends for a while.

The Redditch Advertiser 28 January 2003

REDDITCH TOWN LITTERED WITH TROLLEYS

In all the letters and articles concerned with a "Tidy Redditch" no one mentioned the most obstructive and expensive item of litter – the hundreds of bulky abandoned shopping trolleys (approximate value £100 each) which ornament the town in every direction every day, except for the day of the Queen's visit, when the town centre was clean, with not a trolley in sight.

It seems that this practice will continue because the will to end it does not exist. A few years ago I took a special interest in the "trolley problem" hoping to do something to reduce it, but I was not successful. The then Manager of Sainsbury's, when I approached him, reported that Sainsbury's Head Office stated that a deposit system was at that time against the firm's policy.

I suggest that there should be a deposit of £1 on every trolley used, to cure the problem and will wait to see what action is taken.

The Redditch Advertiser 1st August 1990

TAKING CARE OF THE FOUNTAIN
Church Green, Redditch

… stop the litter

There is nothing more soothing and peaceful than a running brook as it ripples over its pebbles murmuring a quiet tune, or a fountain as it plays in the sunlight. When H M Queen Elizabeth visited Redditch in 1983, the town had been swept and garnished and the fountain on Church Green sparkled on that beautiful day of royal weather.

Now the fountain stands idle. Every time it is turned on, it is not long before the moat around it is choked with debris and the trolleys from people who don't mind losing their £1 deposit.

The Redditch Advertiser 9th January 1992

TROLLEY – CAMPAIGN VICTORY

I note with some degree of wry satisfaction that Tesco's have at length and at last decided to control their trolleys with a deposit system, which was urged by me ten years ago in my one-man campaign! This combined with the Borough Council's decision to collect and impound abandoned trolleys should go a long way towards solving this vexed problem.

The town centre will look better. Will Joe Sainsbury follow suit I wonder?

The Redditch Advertiser 7th November 1991

CARELESS CYCLISTS

The Church Green pedestrian area is often trespassed upon by cyclists who ignore the notices and pedal at speed with no regard for other people and give no warning of their approach. On my morning visits to the town hardly a day passes, but I have to side step some of these cyclists. It used to be customary to carry a bell on your handle bars and in my opinion that should be a legal requirement.

The Arrow Valley Park is another place where cyclists ride. The long footpath around the lake is often used as a cycle track. Some time ago I addressed a letter on this subject to Redditch Town Hall and received a somewhat sympathetic reply. I was hoping that notice boards might carry a request to cyclists to show consideration towards other users of the park but to the best of my knowledge no such action has been taken.

The Redditch Advertiser 18th June 1997

NURSES WITHOUT CAPS

I have been an in-patient at Alexandra Hospital four times in the last two years. One thing I have noticed with regret is the gradual disappearance of the *nurse's cap. My mental picture of these caring angels still includes a starched apron and white cap. On enquiry I was told the cap gets in the way.

The nurses look better with their cap, which to me is almost sacred like the Salvation Army bonnet. Cap or no cap they treated me wonderfully on Ward Seventeen.

The Redditch Advertiser 18th November 1994

*nurses without caps (Ref App G)

ALEXANDRA HOSPITAL
Funding for the CT Scanner 1996

Mr Les Lawrence states that the new CT scanner is an example of the commitment of the Alexandra Hospital to continuously improve its service.

I would also say that it is an example of the commitment of local people to their hospital, since it seems that they raised most of the purchase price of this equipment.

The people of Redditch and Bromsgrove have taken the hospital to their hearts and many (including me) have reason to be grateful for the excellent medical treatment and nursing care.

The Redditch Advertiser 20th November 1996

Chapter 6

Local History:
People, Places And Events

People

"John could be relied upon for realistic and informed comment on a wide range of subjects. His knowledge of the countryside which he loved was unrivalled, and his grasp of history and political problems revealed an alert and probing mind, which would never be satisfied with 'can't' or half-truths."

Roy Webb, Obituary to John Bomford

WILLEM WHITMORE 1870
Review of court proceedings...

Willem Whitmore was once more brought before the bench at Redditch Petty Sessions, charged with being drunk and riotous on the 13th.

He might almost have been committed for riotous conduct in the court before the bench, so impudently defiant was his behavior.

On his name being called he came stumping his wooden leg noisily and calling out:

"Now you may save a lot of reading and bother for I'm going to plead guilty: but I want to know, where's the other? There was two of us."

The clerk then read the charge – and then Willem repeated this, adding "What does 'em take me for, and where's the other? He hit me and I should be a fool if I didn't stand in my own defense."

His persistent course of blackguardism has long since carried him beyond small fines for early offences: in this case the fine was forty shillings and costs nine shillings or one month's imprisonment.

The Redditch Advertiser 29 March 1995

Reply to the editor of the Advertiser by Roy Webb

WILLEM WHITMORE 1870
Court proceedings...

I was interested in your review about Willem Whitmore and his appearance at the Petty Sessions in 1870 for riotous behavior. This drunken ex-sailor lived in a lodging house in Red Lion Street, (now part of the Town Hall site).

Fifty years ago stories were still circulating of his feud with the police and how he would unscrew his wooden leg and use it as a weapon of defense or offence.

*Roy Clews mentions him (anachronistically) in his book "Young Jethro" in connection with the bread riots of 1812.

The Redditch Advertiser 5th April 1995

*(Ref App I)

CARING FOR THE GRAVE
of PC James Davies of Beoley

Memorial for James Davies, St Leonard's Church yard, Beoley © B.K. Watkins.

The letter from Colin Wheeler about the murdered policeman James Davies reminds me of an evening when I met a police constable from Beoley in the Village Inn public house.

The police constable had that day received a telephone call from his Redditch Police Superintendent who ordered him to go immediately to the church yard and tidy up James Davies' grave. This was the result of a complaint from an old lady who had reported its neglected state.

James Davies murder spot is not many yards from the Coach and Horses on Weatheroak Hill. I have seen an old photograph of PC Davies, a tall man of athletic build with mutton chop whiskers.

Shrimpton, the accused perpetrator, was found guilty and was hanged in Worcester Jail on Whit Monday 1885.

The Redditch Advertiser 4th October 1995.

*St Leonard's Church yard, Beoley (Ref App G)

JAMES HENRY STYLER
5th May 1881 – December 1968
(Draper and Haberdasher at 15 Church Green East for 70 years)

James Henry Styler with his wife Henrietta.

Many residents of Redditch will remember my Uncle Harry, James Henry Styler, Draper and Haberdasher at 15 Church Green East for 70 years.

He was born in 1881 the second eldest of a family of thirteen children. In 1897 he was apprenticed to a Draper in Sparkhill for three years on a "living in basis", during which time he was forbidden to drink, gamble or get married.

Returning to Redditch in 1900 he started in business on Church Green East with a loan from his mother (Prudence Styler) to pay for his first year's stock. His premises, formerly a dwelling house were converted into a shop, by knocking the two down stairs rooms into one. A steep spiral staircase was fitted to give access to the living quarters above and increase the area in the shop.

James Henry Styler (Uncle Harry) died in 1968 aged 87 years. The accumulated stock including many unsold items that had lain on his shelves for

Copy of indenture signed by his father Frederick Styler (our grandfather).

years was auctioned off at give-away prices. He lies buried at Edgeoake Lane, Astwood Bank and his shop is now a Building Society Office.

The Redditch Advertiser 2nd January 1992

IN MEMORY OF JOHN BOMFORD, MARLFIELD FARM, BEOLEY
… tribute to a true friend

St Leonard's Church Yard, Beoley © B.K.Watkins.

It is with a heavy heart and a great sense of personal loss that I write this tribute to my friend John Bomford, of Marlfield Farm, Beoley, whose young life has been brought to such a tragic end and who is mourned by a wide circle of friends in many walks of life.

Educated at Redditch County High School, John proceeded to Bangor University for a Degree in Agriculture and to Durham University where he gained his M.Sc.

With his Father, Mr. Ernest Bomford and his brother Raymond, he farmed the 200 acres at Beoley, which are now unhappily to be acquired by the Redditch Development Corporation.

John was a leading member of Redditch Cricket, Hockey and Tennis Club – where he will be long remembered.

His warm heart and unfailing sense of humour endeared him to everyone he met.

Many conversations have been enlivened by his quick flashes of wit. John could be relied upon for realistic and informed comment on a wide range of subjects. His knowledge of the countryside which he loved was unrivalled and his grasp of history and political problems revealed an alert and probing mind, which would never be satisfied with "can't" or half-truths.

My words are inadequate to express his worth; a generous nature, a true gentleman and a staunch friend. To have known him was a privilege.

For me, his cheerful face and kindly greeting will forever be associated with my walks near his home. The memory of John will revive with every gentle shower, every wind that rustles the leaves in Icknield Street, with the sweet smell of every newly-ploughed field, and with every Spring which spreads its green mantle over Beoley Hill.

The Redditch Indicator 21st March 1969

*St Leonard's Church yard, Beoley (Ref App G)

DIANA (Princess of Wales)
... remembering her grave

Brian's White Garden © B Skeys.

Let the heavens embrace her
And wild flowers deck her grave
Violets bright as every shower
Drop diamonds on her bower

When summer sun shines on that quiet place
The rose will shed its petals on her face.

September 1997

IRENE MURIEL WEBB – British Empire Medal
1991 New Years' Honours Awards

Irene M Webb with school children.

The British Empire Medal was awarded to *Irene Muriel Webb, for 35 years of service, working as a School Patrol Crossing Officer for children of St Luke's First School, Plymouth Road, Southcrest, Redditch. Irene made life safer for thousands of children during that time.

Wife of Roy Webb

OBITUARY JESSICA HOUFTON

Surgeon, Councillor, Commandant of the Redditch Branch of the British Red Cross, Justice of the Peace and Chairman of the Bench of Redditch Magistrates Court Jessica Houfton the first woman to be elected to Redditch Urban District Council has died. She was aged 89.

Mrs Houfton trained as a nurse at St Bartholomew's Hospital, London, where she met her husband, Ernest. They acquired a practice in Redditch in 1928 which they ran until 1964.

Dr Houfton was Chief Surgeon in the Borough until the start of the National Health Service. Mrs Houfton was Commandant of the Redditch branch of the British Red Cross for several years, a Justice of the Peace and Chairman of the Bench at Redditch Magistrates Court.

During the war, she helped nurse badly injured servicemen at a Bromsgrove hospital and drove a van to help the war effort by collecting newspapers and jam jars.

Mrs Houfton of Upper Bentley, leaves an adopted daughter, Mollie, two granddaughters – Claire and Jane, and two great grandchildren.

Her funeral service was held at St Bartholomew's Church, Tardebigge.

The Redditch Advertiser 5th May 1993

TRIBUTE TO JESSICA HOUFTON

Having read the obituary on Mrs Jessica Houfton, I would like to add my tribute. I knew Dr and Mrs Houfton when they lived in Worcester Road in the 1930s. Dr Houfton performed an operation on me in 1940 and we remained friends thereafter. Years later, I visited Mrs Houfton several times at her home at Upper Bentley with its lovely rose garden and she was very kind and hospitable.

As Chairman of the Licensing Justices she was held in awe by the local licensees with her insistence on cleanliness in public houses.

It was a privilege to have known a lady with such grace.

Roy Webb

The Redditch Advertiser 12th May 1993

Places

LAW SOCIETY
HOUSE JOURNAL

Dear Sir,

As a native of Redditch, I knew Ipsley when it was a quiet green place consisting of St Peter's Church, the Old Mill, a few scattered farmsteads and cottages and not much else. It puzzled me that a church of such dimensions as St Peter's had no village to go with it. Perhaps the village was destroyed in the 14th Century by the Black Death? No one seems to know.

The church of course, is 12th century and Ipsley Court is reputed to date from 1492. The *Huband family, owners of the Ipsley Estate in Tudor times were friends of Shakespeare. The Court as you probably know was the summer home of the Victorian poet, Walter Savage Landor (born in Leamington) who loved the peace and tranquility of the place. What would he make of it today? The Ipsley estate was sold off in 1921.

In the 1930's Ipsley Court was farmed by Jefferies and later by Morgan, before the Development Corporation arrived in 1964. The following lines are by W S Landor:

"I strove with none, for none was worth my strife;
Nature I loved and next to Nature, Arts;
I warmed my hands before the fire of life,
It sinks and I am ready to depart."
(Written presumably as an old man.)

The Rev Michael Stuart King, the eccentric Irish rector in 1940 of St Peter's Church, delivered violent attacks against Hitler from the pulpit. When a few stray bombs shattered some of the rectory windows, he said, "I knew Hitler had got one for me."

I hope these jottings may be of some interest.

Yours sincerely, Roy Webb

October 1991

**Huband family (Ref App. G)*

HISTORIC IPSLEY

Ipsley Court

In Tudor times it was much extended in the form of a letter "E" for Elizabeth (like many Tudor buildings). Later damaged by fire it has survived in reduced form, and is listed for its historic interest. For three centuries the Huband family at the Court were patrons of the church and owners of the Ipsley estate.

Redditch Advertiser 14th October 1991

Author's Note:

In my brother's comments to the Law Society, he wrote that Ipsley Church appeared not to have a village: I have included the following information by kind permission of Mr. R.H. Richardson and Mr. R. Whittaker.

Richardson, R.H., 'The Administration of the Old Poor Law in *Ipsley, 1797-1804' in *Studies in Worcestershire Local History Vol. 4* (1988**) edited by R.Whittaker.**

"The Tithe Award Map B.A.1572 Ref No 760/370 for 1842 shows Ipsley Parish in 1842 to have been largely rural – no obvious village centre. Ipsley appears to resemble closely many of the small villages of the Arrow Valley where the original settlement around the church and manor house dispersed at some time in the middle ages possibly because of poor soil in the area, for example the Studley people regrouped on Icknield Street half a mile away from the church and castle. Little sign of this at Ipsley. Clearly the original settlement was to the west of St Peter's Church, where a public footpath almost certainly is all that remains of the main street of the village."

*Ipsley, (Ref App. G)

REDDITCH, CIRCA 1840

Who's who…

Edward Browning, Attorney, now Browning & Co

Anglican Chapel of Ease, (1805-1855), now St Stephen's Church

Roman Catholic Church, Beoley Road, opened 1834

Fox & Goose (later the Royal Hotel) a coaching Inn: The Rocket called daily en route from Birmingham to Alcester

Thomas Huins, Shoemaker

William Hollington, Draper

William Whittington, Miller at Ipsley Mill

Barrells Hall, a small stately home near Henley-in-Arden. The Newtons a wealthy local family bought the Barrells Park estate in 1856

Undated

History (Ref App G)

1871 BUILDING ST GEORGE'S CHURCH, REDDITCH 125 YEARS AGO

St George's Church with Author in foreground– 2012 © E Moore.

For many months past the Rev G F Fessey has been quietly at work with a hope to finding the monies to provide a church for the south eastern end of the town. Within the last few weeks he has received such liberal aid as leaves no doubt of ultimate success. From the representatives of the Hewell Estate he has been offered the land measuring half an acre and a donation of £300. The site chosen is the Beoley Lane allotment gardens, a very pleasant place, not far from the entrance to the Beoley Road.

Among many handsome subscriptions we have heard of £200 from Mr. Millward and £100 from the Bartleet family. The subscriptions already arrive at such an amount that the vicar has put himself in touch with the architect, Mr Preedy. The outlay contemplated is about £2,000. The ministry of the church is to be by Curacy to St Stephen's.

Author Unknown

The Redditch Advertiser 24th July 1996

Author's Note

When I visited St George's Church, during the spring of 2012, the church was closed and discussions continue about its sale and use. The closure of this once active church is a great loss to the local parishioners and others from outside the parish who attended the services.

It is a listed building (Ref App. G)

REDDITCH TOWN MARKET

Redditch open market is now a large bustling six day affair and a good source of revenue for the Borough Council, who own the market rights.

In the 1920s, the market tolls were paid to the *Lord of the Manor (the Earl of Plymouth), and consisted of about a dozen market stalls and a few handcarts, on Market Place alongside St Stephen's Church.

"Market Place 1905" – until 1914 our Grandmother (Prudence Styler)
sold meat each Saturday from her market pitch,
(which was opposite J Scott & Son Drapers, identified with a star).

Saturday evening was a busy time when some of the market stalls (especially butchers – who lacked the means of refrigerating unsold meat) were open until midnight and would sell their meat at reduced prices. Customers would come at this time and buy their meat for Sunday lunch the following day. H Ralph did a thriving trade in fruit and vegetables opposite the Old Royal Hotel. Ladbury's sold fresh fish from a handcart, while "Rocky" Herbert's sugar confectionary and golden brown gingerbread glinted under the light of the naphthalene flares which was the main source of illumination.

At the lower end of Market Place there was a German tank, a trophy from World War I. A few yards away in Church Green East, Albert Lejenne, a refugee from war-torn Belgium had a taxi stand. Albert was the proprietor of the first taxi service in Redditch.

The Church and the Green were completely enclosed by iron railings which were taken down for the scrap metal drive in World War II, which in my opinion improved the appearance of the area. Woolworths (now Tony's Handyman) opened in the early 1930s and was, I believe, the first purpose built store in the town, the other shops being house conversions.

The Redditch Advertiser 10th October 1991

WARWICKSHIRE AND WORCESTERSHIRE CHURCH AND PARISH RECORDS

To those of a sardonic turn of mind, much can be gleaned from ancient churches and their records (both written and engraved) about the "tragic comedy" of life. The "smile", prompted by quaint inscriptions in country churchyards and entries in Parish Registers, is quickly quenched with a "melancholy sigh". So much for rhetoric, let me come down to earth with a few examples.

A Warwickshire church contains a marble tablet to the memory of a local squire of illustrious birth who, as a young man, studied Law at the Inns of Court. The fulsome eulogy explains that having been called to the Bar, the possession of an ample fortune, caused him to retire to the no less useful life as a Country Gentleman. This arduous pursuit occupied him for half a century, and he died deeply mourned. Another Warwickshire church informs visitors of a Charity, with income secured on the rent of a field, for the Relief of the Poor of the Parish, especially needy widows of good character, through the provision of coals and blankets.

Parish Registers sometimes carry marginal notes inserted by the Vicar. An entry of burial dated 1817 in a Worcestershire church states:

"A poor unknown man aged about 33, who died of a fever."

The Baptismal register in the same church has several entries in the name of a spinster from a cottage on a neighbouring hill, she followed the scriptural injunction "to be fruitful and multiply". Her illegitimate children were all charitably baptised by the vicar. Another unfortunate parishioner was "Buried on Coroner's Warrant, having shot himself."

Finally, an epitaph to a mole catcher, for which I cannot vouch, which runs as follows:

"Here lies the body of Tandy,
He was very handy at catching moles,
In every hole he caught a mole,
At the last the hole caught Tandy."

Author unknown

17th September 1976

History Records (Ref Apps G, H and I)

REVIEWING GRAVEYARDS IN REDDITCH

"Three things in human life are important: the first is to be kind; the second is to be kind; and the third is to be kind."
Henry James (15.04.1843 – 28.02.1916)

There are still a few old gravestones in St Stephen's church yard. When, I wonder, was the last person buried there, presumably when the "old" cemetery in Plymouth Road became available to use. The "old" cemetery contains the mortal remains of many local people some with elaborate head-stones and fulsome epitaphs, and others are more modest. Since the war, the Abbey Cemetery has been in use.

In 1964, there was a small graveyard in Evesham Street, which was in front of the Congregational Church. This is no longer in use – the most recent inscription is 100 years old. The Evesham Street graveyard is now occupied by Owen Owen's Store, and (according to some reports) haunted by the occasional ghost.

The Redditch Advertiser 2nd January 1992
History (Ref Apps G, H, I)

BORDESLEY ABBEY – ARCHEOLOGICAL DIGS, 1991

I have read a report that the archeological digs at *Bordesley Abbey have produced a quantity of tiles, fragments of masonry, skeletons, etc and that these artefacts are to be sent all over the country to be examined by experts. How much of this will be lost?

The Abbey Meadows are part of Arrow Valley Park and all such finds are the property of the town and people of Redditch. It would be safer if the artefacts could be retained for display in the Abbey Museum.

15th August 1991

*Bordesley Abbey (Ref App. G)

PROSPECT HILL, REDDITCH

I read with interest that W T Heming founder of the "Redditch Indicator" has his printing premises on Prospect Hill.

This must explain "Heming's Entry", a quiet footpath linking Prospect Hill and Clive Road, which was a popular meeting place for courting couples in the 1920s and 30s.

The Redditch Advertiser 29th September 1999

THE BAPTIST CHURCH, REDDITCH

The Baptist Church in Easemore Road (Memory Lane article published June 10) can hardly be called a "turn of the century building". It was opened in 1921 and took the place of the original Baptist Church acquired by Herbert Terry & Sons manufacturers of springs. The mansion built at Southcrest by Charles Terry was also completed in 1921.

My mother a war widow who had married her first husband in the old Baptist Church in October 1914, was awarded a pension of two shillings (10p) per week. She also received a medallion from Buckingham Palace which carried a message of sympathy from the then King George V and Queen Mary.

The Redditch Advertiser 17th June 1998

Research Source (Ref App. G)

HISTORY OF PLACE NAMES IN THE REDDITCH AREA

In response to Dennis Crate about local history names here is some information which may help.

Headless Cross and Crabbs Cross

The four place names he mentions have origins far older than the Redditch Development Corporation and the town planners of the 1960s. In 1964 Headless Cross and Crabbs Cross were small villages each about three centuries old; like many old place names the true explanation is obscure. It is recorded that in 1651 a certain Colonel Crabb mustered a force of men and marched them off to the Battle of Worcester. "Headless" may have started out as "Hedley's Cross" that is a man's name.

Winyates

"Winyates" was the name of a farm adjacent to the old Rectory at Ipsley, until it was built over. This name is not peculiar to Redditch. A Tudor house in South Warwick is called Compton Winyates.

Moons Moat

The neighbourhood now known as "Moons Moat" has for its focus a small pool which is a scheduled monument, being "Lord Moon's Moat". I have no information on Lord Moon, but the place is the reputed site of the legendary Sheldon treasure – the wealthy family who introduced the art of tapestry weaving into England in the mid-16th century, and whose chapel can be seen in St Leonard's Church, Beoley.

3rd October 1999

History (Ref App G)

REMEMBERING "GRAFTON HOUSE"

Sixty years ago in a quiet road just off the main shopping street of a small town, stood a roomy Victorian house, a comfortable dignified place where no one ever raised their voice and life followed a tranquil routine. A huge grandfather clock stood in a corner of the breakfast room, and an elegant grandmother clock, which was set to chime on every quarter of the hour, graced the upstairs landing.

The lawned garden was enclosed by a high brick wall. How peaceful and secluded it was for a town house, divided from the back yard by a green trellised fence and gate.

The lawn was the setting for leisurely tea parties, presided over by the gentle old lady who kept the house, with the use of the Summer House if the weather was unpromising.

Peacock butterfly © B Skeys.

Herbaceous borders were gay with butterflies and flowers and alive with bees. Sparrows twittered in the ivy on the back wall and a single tall tree produced green cooking apples. One warm afternoon a swarm of bees flew into the garden and settled in a velvet cluster hanging onto a branch of the tree. In winter the nimble blue-tits would perch on coconut shells, strings of monkey nuts or pieces of fat which hung from the trellis.

This garden was two minutes' walk from the church and two minutes from the railway station in the other direction. Where was it – in some Cathedral city or sleepy Spa? No, it stood where the basement of Sainsbury's new empty supermarket now stands, in the Kingfisher Mall. It was "Grafton House", 25 Worcester Road, which doubtless other older residents of Redditch will recall.

The Redditch Advertiser 21st February 1990

Tree sparrow, House Sparrow RSPB breeding decline long-term BDp2**Red status** *Blue-tit RSPB* Green status *(Ref App. F)*

Bees: Endangered species (Ref App. F) state of nature *(Ref App. G)*

Author's Note:

My brother visited "Grafton House" with our parents and my two sisters, where our Aunt, Florence E Webb was companion help to Emily Jane Ball who lived there.

A JOURNEY DOWN THE RIVER ARROW
By Pam Newbold

I was interested in Pam Newbold's account of the new video "A Journey down the River Arrow". This river was re aligned by Redditch Development Corporation from Beoley Brook to Ipsley. Natives of old Redditch will remember this stretch as the Race Course Meadows, and the Arrow now runs alongside the west bank of the Arrow Valley Lake but to the best of my knowledge, does not feed it.

The lake in fact is supplied by a smaller stream from Holt End, Beoley, which crosses Icknield Street near Brooklyn Garages and enters the lake on its eastern side. It emerges at the Ipsley end and flows on to join the Arrow near the site of Ipsley Mill, now demolished.

The Arrow is twenty miles in length, and used to boast 20 Water Mills. It joins the Warwickshire Avon at Marlcliff, Bidford on Avon.

The Redditch Advertiser 5th June 1996

Conservation (Ref App E)

THE RIVER ARROW AND HER MILLS, REDDITCH

THE RIVER ARROW
Though only 20 miles in length is notable for the number of mills it supported, producing mainly needles.

FORGE MILL
Now a museum is said to be the only remaining water powered needle mill in the world. Opened by the H M Queen Elizabeth on her visit to Redditch some years ago (when she also opened Milward Square) it is a Visitors' Centre and Museum housing the archeological finds from BORDESLEY ABBEY. These discoveries have received much attention from Birmingham University and other places. This Cistercian Foundation was demolished in 1538 by Henry VIII, after occupying the site for 400 years. The new museum, due to open in November, is an attractive "old-looking" building reconstructed from an ancient barn, which was dismantled and moved to the Abbey Meadows from Matchborough Hill (near Ipsley). With its arches and cloisters it has a monastic atmosphere.

THE PAPER MILL
Before the 2nd World War was still producing paper, and now converted into flats, although its external appearance has been kept, since it is a "listed" building.

IPSLEY MILL
Of course, has gone along with its Mill Pond, and the river follows a different course from the one we knew from Beoley Brook to Ipsley and Washford; having been diverted and straightened by the Development Corporation.

WASHFORD MILL
Just North of Studley is a large rambling place with uneven floors of oak planks. Its mill wheel still rotating inside a glass case is one of its features. It is now a licensed restaurant, its walls covered with nostalgic pictures.

Undated

Conservation (Ref App E)

History (Ref Apps G, H and I)

HARVINGTON at Lilac time
May 1939

Lilac © Brian Skeys

One day in May in thirty-nine
I travelled on the Ashchurch line
By Alcester, Broom and Salford Priors
To Harvington at lilac time

The perfumed sprays of purple flowers
The little station did embower,
With diamond drops the petals glistened
From a sudden gentle shower

Though cares lay heavy on my breast
While the steam train stood at rest,
In Harvington at lilac time
I saw the lilac at its best.

Undated

RAVENSBANK

Dear Sir,

Ravensbank now threatened by the London and Edinburgh Trust (LET) must be an ancient name probably derived from Ravensmere, a small farm which stood a short distance to the east of the present Church Hall Centre.

I have seen no ravens there, but plenty of yellowhammers, barn owls, peewits and rooks (from the Rookery at the top of Beoley Hill). Also rabbits, hares, and badgers. Before 1964, the parish of Beoley with its many *Marl Pits had a high population of badgers. An old deep sett was the one on the western slope of Beoley Hill, on the edge of the spinney behind St Leonard's Church. This impressive sett had a large entrance and several side tunnels. It is probably still there but I do not know whether the badgers have deserted it. But this I do know, these animals on their nocturnal excursions would cross the road to Church Hill Farm, and visit the cornfields of Ravensbank in search of field mice, voles and young rabbits. One day I found a stretch of flattened herbage beneath a hedgerow, and from there I could follow the badger's tracks into the standing corn.

The London Edinburgh Trust are conservationists who will take great pains to preserve the environment.

29th August 1991

Raven RSPB Green status *Barn Owl RSPB* Amber status *(Ref App. F)*
Water vole: one of Britain's most endangered species, (Ref App. F) state of nature
*Marl: A fine ground sedimentary rock consisting of clay minerals, calcite or aragonite and silt, used as fertilizer.

Author's Note: Recipient of letter unknown.

BEAUTIFUL NORGROVE, REDDITCH

As a native of Redditch who has "seen a few summers", I am well aware of the natural beauties of the Norgrove area. I have heard the full throated rhapsody of a nightingale at midnight in a quiet copse near Norgrove Court. I have gathered fragrant white violets from the ivy clad banks in Botters Hill Lane. One Saturday afternoon a large stoat crossed my path at Lower Grinsty to disappear into the hedgerow.

In the past when Canada geese were less common in these parts a small flock of these birds descended on Green Lanes farm in a snowstorm.

On a magical May evening the hedgerows between Lower Grinsty and Callow Hill, were alive with bees, all busy pollinating the flowers of the many holly bushes and trees, and their loud buzzing was clearly audible.

Bee on Sedum flowers © B Skeys.

I am saddened at the loss of this area to development.

18th July 1991

Norgrove Court: built c1649 for William Cookes (Ref App. G)

Nightingale RSPB Amber status (Ref App F)

Bees: Endangered species – see "British Beekeepers Association" and "Worcestershire Beekeepers", (Ref App. F) state of nature (Ref App. G)

Events

BLACK DOG OF ARDEN

Roy Webb writes:

There have been reports that a large "Panther like" animal has been seen near Bordesley Golf Course. I suggest this may be the fabled Black Dog of Arden which has been around for nearly 700 years.

The Redditch Advertiser 24th August 1996

The Author writes:

"Black Dog of Arden" was the nickname bestowed upon Guy de Beauchamp the 10th Earl of Warwick by the arrogant Piers Gaveston, Earl of Cornwall who was King Edward II's favourite. It seems that the Earl was so enraged by this, that he swore that the insolent man should one day "feel his teeth". Piers Gaveston was captured by the Earl of Warwick, taken to Warwick Castle tried by an unofficial court and found guilty of treason. On 1st July 1312 he was taken to Blacklow Hill and beheaded.

The 10th Earl of Warwick died in 1315 and was buried by the monks at Bordesley Abbey, of which monastery he was a patron.

History (Ref App G)

CRIME AND PUNISHMENT 1867

The recent "Down Memory Lane" article described the *punishment in 1867 to an unfortunate Studley man, who received six years penal servitude for forging two Bills of Exchange with a total value of £117. This was a harsh sentence and typical of that era. Many of today's sentences are so lenient as to be ludicrous.

We are reminded of "Poobah" in Gilbert and Sullivan's Opera, "The Mikado" when singing:

"My object all sublime
I shall achieve in time
To let the punishment fit the crime
The punishment fit the crime…"

The Redditch Advertiser 19th March 1992
Victorian Crime & Punishment (Ref App. G)

LOCAL MURDER in the early 1900s

A discussion between D Sly and D Broughton to The Redditch Advertiser, with a reply from Roy Webb:

LOCAL MURDER

I wonder if any reader could give an account of a local murder which I believe occurred in the early 1900s. I remember my late mother telling me about it, but I have forgotten the persons involved.

This murder took place at Foxlydiate. It occurred in either a cottage or a house. Rumour has it that the wife said to her husband, "I'm frizzling you a bit of bacon for your tea," and he replied, "Yes, and I am going to frizzle you tonight." He got drunk and set fire to the place with his wife inside. I believe he was charged with murder and hanged. Can anyone corroborate this?

D Sly

TALE OF MURDER

Reference the letter from Mr Sly. I remember my mother telling me about it. The lady who was murdered and my grandmother lived next door to each other. Every day they both walked to work from Foxlydiate to the bottom of Beoley Road. The story goes that he indeed did go home drunk, killed his wife and roasted her. I remember being told a rhyme after it happened, it goes as follows:

"Her name was Middleton
The policeman who caught him was Billington
He was caught at Himbleton."

I hope that the above information is of some help.

D Broughton

MURDER AND TRIAL

In reply to the letters from Mr Sly and Mr Broughton, many years ago one of my uncles told me about the Foxlydiate murder.

The unfortunate woman apparently was employed at Beoley Paper Mill, in which case she had a long walk to work each day. Her husband having fired the cottage with his wife inside it, made his way to Liverpool hoping to escape the country but was apprehended on the dock side and brought back to face trial and in due course was hanged.

I believe my uncle said that the police officer who arrested this man was a member of our family.

Roy Webb

The Redditch Advertiser 12th October 1995

COURTS MARTIAL World War I

Mr Horner says that the 307 British soldiers shot for cowardice in World War I were all tried by Courts Martial. My late Uncle, Sydney Styler, *M.M., who served as an ambulance man in France in World War I, told me of a Junior Officer who gave the 'over the top' order to a group of men in the trenches. They all obeyed except for one man who started to run away. Having repeated the order to no effect, it seems that the officer drew his revolver and shot him dead on the spot.

Letter unpublished

6th June 1997

World War I – information on soldiers refusing to obey an order (Ref App. G)

*M. M. – Military Medal (Ref App. G)

REDDITCH POETRY CIRCLE 1940

It was stated in a recent issue of the Redditch Advertiser, that the Redditch Society was formed in 1945. The Redditch Society is the off spring of the Redditch Poetry Circle which was active in 1940. The Redditch Poetry Circle meetings took place in the schoolroom of the Congregational Church in Evesham Street.

One evening in October or November 1940, in the absence of a visiting speaker, I delivered a lecture to this small group while German planes droned overhead, on their way to *Birmingham, which was heavily bombed that night.

The Redditch Advertiser 15th September 1993

*Blitz of Birmingham (Ref App. G)

A MEETING OF THE HUNT AT
HATTON HALL, REDDITCH

It was a bright frosty November day and the West Warwickshire Farmers' Foxhounds were meeting at Hatton Hall four miles north of Warwick at 11 a.m. This was a "lawn meet" at the home of Mr S Arkwright, the Master of Foxhounds. A friend and I cycled through the then quiet lanes via Earlswood, Hockley Heath and Chadwick End to arrive at Hatton Hall at about 10.45 a.m. The horses, hounds and riders on the smooth lawns of this imposing house presented a colourful sight.

A silver haired butler appeared with a silver tray carrying glasses of port and sherry, and everyone was graciously offered a (*"stirrup-cup") including my friend and I, who each enjoyed a sherry.

Foxhunting is a cruel sport which I have long ceased to support, but I remember Hatton Hall with pleasure.

The Redditch Advertiser 23rd July 1992

Stirrup-cup – a drink offered to the hunts man, before commencing the hunt.

Author's Note: See UK Hunting Act 2004 banning hunting.

1964 YEAR OF CHANGE FOR REDDITCH

In the saga of Redditch the year 1964 seems almost as significant as 1066. A tidal wave of development engulfed the town and swept away streets in the town centre, among them Worcester Road, which gave its name to Worcester Square. Worcester Road ran from the Talbot Public House in Evesham Street to Park Road and the railway station. Below the Talbot stood the Temperance Hall (later the Kingfisher Hall) which was the headquarters of the total abstainers who had renounced the "Demon Drink". There used to be an annual procession of "little white ribboners" – children who had been persuaded to sign the pledge. The rest of this short road consisted mainly of substantial middle class Victorian houses (in contrast to the many sub-standard dwellings in the neighbourhood, for example, Hill Street, Walford Street and Red Lion Street). It was the "Harley Street" of Redditch. Several well remembered doctors resided there including Dr John Campbell Dow, who had three sons, the eldest of whom Thomas Dow (also a doctor) was at school with me in the 1930s.

I noticed today (September 21) the existence of Doctor Dow House in William Street where a physician of the same name is a member of the practice. If Dr Dow House is to set a precedent I am reminded of another former Redditch partnership – Drs Potts and Chambers.

The Redditch Advertiser 21st September 1995

Listed buildings (Ref App. G)

BATTLE OF BRITAIN DAY

On the morning of Monday, September 15 (Battle of Britain Day) I noticed the Union Jack flying bravely from the flagpole above Redditch Town Hall, on enquiry, I was told this was for Prince Harry's birthday. I also found that no-one on the streets was collecting money for Royal Air Force charities. Have people forgotten what was achieved by "The Few" in their Spitfires and Hurricanes aircraft in that fateful year of 1940?

Military (Ref App. G)

The Redditch Advertiser 24th September 1997

Chapter 7

The English Language

... Letters

"All the great things are simple, and many can be expressed in a single word: freedom, justice, honour, duty, mercy, hope."

Winston Churchill (30.11.1874 – 24.01.1965)

THE LITURGY IN ANGLICAN CHURCHES

There has recently been much lively correspondence in the Redditch Indicator letters' page about services in Anglican Churches. I hope this belated contribution may be of some interest.

In general young people appear to favour trendy things, like *"Series 3" while their elders regret the abandonment of Cranmer's Common Prayer and the Authorised Version of the Bible. To me, these two books are the cornerstones of the Anglican faith and liturgy. The Order of Services and Lessons appointed for the day is laid down in detail in the Book of Common Prayer. I used to think the guidance provided by these documents had the "force of law", and I wish this were so now.

The Authorised Version of the Bible when first published, was an immediate best seller. And it still is after more than 100,000,000 copies have been sold and no book has had a greater impact on English speaking people the world over. It was taken to North America and elsewhere by thousands of emigrants from these shores. They prized and understood it well enough, and most of them had no formal education. Is our grasp of our "mother tongue" less than that of our "rude" forefathers?

Later translations have destroyed much of the poetry and majesty of the language, without adding greatly to its clarity. It has been watered down by scholars, anxious not to alienate, a generation conditioned to commercial TV and some styles of newspaper reporting. Many rejected expressions have been part of our everyday speech for generations and our language is enriched by them. Why throw away the baby with the bath water?

The complaint that much of the language is obscure or archaic is exaggerated. Some words are adequate others have changed their meaning. But most of them, when read in context, are intelligible to the thoughtful reader.

The Book of Common Prayer is a liturgical gem, containing few words that are long or truly obsolete. I have never been bored by its weekly repetition, or failed to be uplifted and comforted by it. Evensong is a spiritual delight and a poetic masterpiece. The Magnificat the canticle of the Blessed Virgin Mary does more to elevate womanhood than anything else I know.

These two books have stood the test of time and are engraved upon the minds of millions who are dismayed to see them changed.

The Redditch Indicator February 1979

"Series 3" (Ref App. G)

FAMILIAR TERMS OF EXPRESSION

Everyone has heard of the "fatted calf" in the parable of the Prodigal Son (Gospel of Luke (Luke 15:11-32)), I read recently that a professor and his scholastic team were bothered about that. A list of alternative expressions was compiled and shown to a porter at Smithfield, London's meat market.

Asked for his opinion, he said: "Guv, I wouldn't use any of these. We call them 'fatted calves'."

Anyone who is prepared to read the best of English literature from Shakespeare onwards – with a good dictionary at his elbow – will discover a source of perennial interest, and gain an insight into the development of our language.
1979

THE POCKET OXFORD DICTIONARY

Dr Dillon Thompson, Managing Editor
POD Oxford University Press
37a St Giles'
Oxford OX1 3LD

6 July 1992

Dear Dr Thompson,

I am now in possession of the 1992 Edition of the Pocket Oxford Dictionary (POD), a birthday present from my wife. I am delighted with it. Being up to date, it enabled me to clear all the new words and expressions that I had listed in the last 2/3 years. For instance, I wondered why "soap operas" are so-called. Now I know.

This is a masterly work of compression, clarity and compendiousness. The ordinary person needs nothing bigger. And how you can offer it at the low price of £6.99 is beyond me.

My interest in dictionaries began in the 1930s. As a student at Redditch County High School, with a thirst for English literature, I began to encounter many words which were new to me, especially when I embarked upon sixth form English as a principal subject for the Oxford Higher School Certificate.

Redditch at that time was a small town with one inadequate bookshop, but one day I spotted a newspaper advertisement for the Shorter Oxford English Dictionary, which I bought on hire purchase. When it was delivered by the railway parcels wagon, I was amazed at the size of this two volume "Shorter" Dictionary, which proved more than equal to my needs at school.

My first POD (now soiled from much use) was purchased in 1974, and has been an essential book, referred to almost daily, and now its successor will continue the process of my education.

Sincerely,
Roy Webb

Chapter 8

Birds

*Andy Harvey Song Thrush
(rspb-images.com) copyright protected.*

BIRD-SONG IN SPRINGTIME

As the cuckoo calls from the misty fields
Decked with the flowers of another spring,
In new-green hedges small birds sing
Heavily hung with the scented May.
And the speckled thrush's roundelay
May be heard from the orchard bough

And when you get to Beoley Hill
Rooks leave their wind-tossed trees
To wheel around the ancient church
Then set my feet on the old quiet lane
To follow the way I was wont to go
In sunshine, showers or wintry snow.

Along the brook where the pebbles are smooth
Whose gentle murmur my spirit will soothe,
And the wind in the trees has a message for me
While the skylark pours its rhapsody.

2004
Cuckoo and Skylark RSPB BDp 2 **Red status**

SONG OF THE YELLOW HAMMER

Chris Gomersall Yellow Hammer (rspb-images.com). Copyright protected.

"A little bit of bread and no cheese" –
He flutters up between the trees,
And sings his joyful roundelay
on a sweet bright morning in May.

"A little bit of bread and no cheese" –
Uprising on the gentle breeze,
He carols all my cares away
on a sweet bright morning in May.

Above the hedge his quivering wings
Hover in the sunlit air
A sight the heart and eye to please
on a sweet bright morning in May.

1936

The Yellow Hammer, RSPB breeding decline long term BDp2 **Red status**

(Ref. App. F) Give Nature a Home

GARDEN VISITORS IN WINTER

At this time of the year, when few leaves remain, the birds may be seen more clearly and even the most zealous gardener may welcome them, for they can do little damage now. As the winter progresses, scarcity of food brings some of the bolder species closer to human habitations so that a supply of scraps, and a dish of water in frosty weather, will provide you with good entertainment. It is interesting to see the behaviour of the different kinds of birds and the antics of the individual in a flock.

Goldfinches in Brian's garden in January 2013 © B Skeys.

Now that they have recovered from the summertime cares of raising a family, the adult birds have a sleeker appearance; indeed, the plumage of our most common birds is worth our notice. The house sparrows are always with us, but few people appreciate that the male is a very smart fellow. The starlings, whose daily assembly in the tree at the bottom of the garden marks the passing of the winter afternoon, cannot be described as drab, when the green-purple-black of their feathers becomes speckled with white.

Then we have the birds who come singly or in twos and threes. Those acrobats, the blue-tits, will give a splendid performance in return for a suspended morsel, watch for the larger one with a black strip down its tummy, which shows it to be a great-tit. Most members of the thrush family "want to be alone". The cheery robin will fight to the death in defence of its territory.

You are suffered in what you think is your garden, for the sake of worms that your spade brings to the surface, but you will often find yourself under stern supervision. The song thrush, mistle-thrush and blackbird, although more retiring than their small cousins, will gather with the mixed flock at the bird-table when insects and grubs are unobtainable. If you see a thrush of odd appearance, note it carefully, for it may be a winter visitor to this country, a Redwing or possibly a Fieldfare. Both birds will visit gardens throughout the winter, especially if you have windfall apples or throw out some chopped fruit. So as you go about your winter tasks, in the gloom of November or the frosts of January, occasionally lift your gaze from the earth and see the lively company that lightens the sadness of a garden without flowers.

Circa 1968

Song Thrush, House Sparrow, Tree Sparrow, Starling, Redwing and Fieldfare: RSPB Breeding decline long-term BDp2**Red status**

(see more from RSPB in App. F)

Goldfinch, Blackbird, Robin, Blue tit, and Great tit: RSPB Green status

WILD FLOWERS FOR YOUR GARDEN
Some jottings...

Wild Geranium © Emery Moore.

Consider that the dandelion, handsome and irrepressible, has many useful properties, not the least of which is the home-made wine that induces oblivion without enriching the Chancellor of the Exchequer. However, I cannot seriously plead for it as a garden subject, having tried for twenty years to rid a small front garden of its tenacious roots. Every year, in May, it lifts its golden head and laughs at me.

But who will deny the beauty of the mallow, with its mauve-striped petals and quaintly segmented leaves? This cousin of the hollyhock was held in high esteem by the old herbalists. It would never be a weed in my garden, but it never grows there. Instead, it flourishes on a rough untended bank in the local bus station, where on this date (16th July) there is a profusion of bloom from scores of plants.

My thoughts turn to wiry harebells, spiked toadflax, and the magnificent meadow crane's-bill – the wild geranium of the Cotswolds, but these, the true wildings, too shy and elusive to invade our plots, are the work of the divine alchemist, who has no weeds in his garden.

Circa 1968

THE ISLE IS FULL OF NOISES

Lapwing (peewit) Andy Hay (rspb-images.com) copyright protected.

As I stand at my bedroom window my eyes travel slowly over the Arden countryside which lies to the South-East. It is quiet, well wooded and faintly mysterious, a green sea breaking gently on the hard edges of the "New" Redditch, which gradually invades the near fields and the middle distance. My gaze moves from Outhill to Morton Bagot, from Mappleborough Green to Spernal Park, and I wonder about those people at Shelfield, whose slumbers are "disturbed" by the cries of wild birds and animals, while there are others who live daily with the noise of machinery. I don't suppose I shall ever hear again from my front garden the mating call of a pair of peewits as they tumbled over each other in a cold bright February sky. All the peewits have gone to Shelfield. I saw 50 of them myself the other day in a newly ploughed field near Little Alne in the company of a tall grey heron, which floated upwards when it saw me and flew with unhurried grace in the direction of Wootton Wawen.

The Grey Heron © photograph by Richard Newton.

By the time I reached home I was almost "deafened" by the noise of falling acorns and the wind rustling the leaves on the autumn painted trees. Let an earlier inhabitant of Arden have the last word, and redeem my faltering sentences:

> "Art thou afeard? Be not afeard
> The Isle is full of noises
> Sounds and sweet airs
> Which give delight and hurt not."
> William Shakespeare – The Tempest, Caliban to Stephano.
> 23.04.1564 – 23.04.1616

The Redditch Indicator 7th November 1969

Lapwing, RSPB Red status, Grey heron, RSPB **Green status** *(Ref App. F)*

Arden (Ref App. B)

THE BLUE TIT
... feeding habits

Blue tit © Photograph by Richard Newton.

In summertime I'm in the woods
In leafy glade and glen,
But when the frost is on the grass
I haunt the homes of men.

I peck the shells of coco-nuts,
And swing around with ease,
My acrobatic tricks would shame
Gymnasts on their trapeze.

In early morn the milkman calls,
I'm waiting there unseen
To pierce the golden bottle-tops
And drink the topmost cream.

At eight o'clock the housewife comes
And finds her bottle slit,
But still she likes to watch me
A nimble little tit.

September 1976
Blue tit RSPB Green Status *(Ref App. F)*

SPARROWS AND MEN

Sparrow. Ray Kennedy (rspb-images.com) copyright protected.

Whilst sitting on Church Green one day
Having a bite to eat,
A cheeky sparrow left the grass
And hopped up to my feet.

The flower-beds made a bright display,
The sun shone through the trees,
To me it was a lovely day
But he was after bread and cheese.

Bold and careful both at once,
He did not come too near,
But lost no time in pecking up
The crumbs I scattered there.

Ere long a score of other birds
Had joined him in a rush,
Mostly sparrows, young and old,
Two starlings and a thrush.

All were cautious, some were brave,
The front rank took the bread,
To be pursued by those behind
Who stole from them and fled.

This seemed to me to illustrate
Something of human fate,
When those who do the work
May be robbed by those who wait.

October 1976
House Sparrow, Tree Sparrow RSPB breeding decline long term BDp2 **Red status**
(Ref App. F)

PIGEON WARFARE

To me as a native of Redditch the feral pigeons on Church Green are a fairly recent arrival. They give me pleasure although they are viewed with disfavour by some of the shop keepers.

Recently while walking past St Stephen's Church my ears were assailed by the noise of conflict. A battle was raging between the pigeons and a band of black invader – jackdaws, who were evidently looking for roosting places in the church spire. Feathers were being lost and harsh cries accompanied this territorial dispute. It makes a change from the usual hustle and bustle of the town.

To the small group of readers who I know enjoy my occasional letters I wish you, "A More Peaceful New Year".

The Redditch Advertiser 3rd January 1996

Jackdaw RSPB Green Status *(Ref App. F)*

SIGHTING A KESTREL WAS A RARE PRIVILEGE

Kestrel photograph © Richard Newton.

As an amateur naturalist who remembers when nightingales sang in Rough Hill Wood, I have been saddened by the loss of bird life in Redditch since 1964 when the Development Corporation began the huge changes to the town and its surrounding area. It is years since I saw a swallow and the peewits have long since sought pastures new.

You will, therefore, imagine my delight this morning in Ipsley Street, when a Kestrel (*Hover Hawk*) touched down on the pavement a yard from me. He rose quickly and *scythed his way to a clump of trees. A rare sighting of this beautiful bird of prey!

A thought too about the sparrow

These days there are too many egg stealing magpies and a consequent decline in the number of small birds, including the once ubiquitous sparrow which I regret. What is life without the cheerful sparrow in our streets and our gardens?

The Redditch Advertiser 29th July 1996

*scythed – with a curve

House sparrow, Tree sparrow RSPB breeding decline long-term BDp2 *Red status Kestrel, Swallow RSPB* Amber status *Magpie RSPB* Green status *(Ref App F)*

MAGPIES ON GUARD

Roy's Cherry Trees. Planted c 1960.

In early May our back garden was sown with grass seed, and I was apprehensive that flocks of marauding birds would descend each morning and use the plot as a source of breakfast cereal. But the winged invasion did not take place. A pair of magpies had a nest in a hawthorn tree in the garden. Every other bird that appeared was chased away; the garden remained quiet and we have a flourishing new lawn.

30th June 1991

Magpie RSPB Green status *(Ref App F)*

Chapter 9

Conservation

Blackbird.

Green woodpecker.

Bluebell.

THE ENCHANTED COTTAGE

"Faerie contains many things besides elves and fays, and besides dwarfs, witches, trolls, giants, or dragons; it holds the seas, the sun, the moon, the sky; and the earth, and all things that are in it: tree and bird, water and stone, wine and bread, and ourselves, mortal men, when we are enchanted."

J.R.R. Tolkien (03.01.1892 – 02.09.1973)

When I was a boy I visited the cottage where my grandfather had lived on the Slough near Studley Station. The visits took me into another world, away from Redditch which seemed like a big city.

The cottage in its completeness with nature was enchanting. The wood opposite was full of singing birds including the nightingale. There were foxes,*red squirrels and many rabbits. A gate from the cottage garden led into a small meadow with a spinney at the bottom which was by a stream.

It was magical.

The Redditch Advertiser 18 May 1994

Nightingale RSPB amber status

The *red squirrel is a protected species in the UK (Ref App F) state of nature

SPRING FLOWERS

Primular Vulgaris © B Skeys.

Now is the time of birdsong clear
And urgent at the break of day,
Of silken drapes, upon the larch,
And fragrant violets in the way.
There is a symphony of gold
Primrose clumps and daffodils,
Willow plumes and celandines,
And sunlight on the misty hills.

4th April 1957

APRIL SHOWERS

It's morning and the kindly sun
With golden fingers warms the air,
Dissolves the mists of early rain
And frees my mind from care.

Daffodils © B Skeys.

Raindrop-drops, glistening, fall from leaves
And patter softly on my head,
So in this gentle sacrament
The demons from the soul are fled.

On summer fields of green and gold
The sun's caress in ardour grows,
And when the bugler blackbird calls
The eager heart a new joy knows.

In every tiny leaf and root
Life renewed, relentless springs,
And hope that languished in the night
Is one with countless growing things.

4th April 1957
Blackbird RSPB Green Status *(Ref App. F)*

FALLING IN LOVE WITH WEEDS
"To me, the meanest flower that blows can give
Thoughts that do often lie too deep for tears."
William Wordsworth 07.04.1770 – 23.04.1850

Yellow Rattle or Cockscomb (Rhinanthus minor) © B Skeys.

A weed, we are told, is a plant growing in the wrong place. In gardens this results in the ruthless eradication of every representative of our own flora, in favour of gaudy flowers from sun-baked veldt or the rocky vastness of Nepal. Some of our native plants are rampant and unlovely, but all are condemned because they are commonplace, and all are excluded to make room for "weeds" from other lands. Drunk with the showy splendour of intruders from the Antipodes, we overlook the merits of our own wildings (*wild flowers*).

The convolvulus, or bindweed, haunts the dreams of gardeners, springing as it does from untold depths on serpentine roots, every inch of which is pregnant with the urge to grow and throw up bines (*climbing stems*) to meet the sun. Prodigious feats of digging have been directed towards its overthrow. A large fork is the tool for the operation. Jobbing gardeners use a spade, which ensures both the propagation of the weed and the continuance of their own employment. This is a climbing plant whose powers of encroachment are exaggerated. It is relatively easy to confine it to the boundary fence or hedge, where it will reward your tolerance with a noble display of white trumpets in the summer – far superior, in my opinion, to the undistinguished Convolvulus Minor, on which I expended a few pence one year.

The Scarlet Pimpernel appears to be a harmless little plant, although domestic poultry will not eat it, and are not to be deceived into taking it for chickweed. The poor man's weather-glass, as it is known, closes its petals when rain is imminent. Not a reliable guide, for the petals are always closed after about 2.00 p.m.

Circa 1968

Conservation (Ref App E)

AN OLD PROVERB ABOUT DAISIES
"When you can put your foot on three daisies spring is come."
Author unknown

St Leonard's Church, Beoley © B.K.Watkins.

Surely spring has few equals in its warmth, its colour, and natural beauty.

A recent walk in the countryside near Redditch revealed much to gladden the eye and cheer the heart. Never was the grass so green and fresh, the air so clear and wholesome to the lungs, the breeze so gentle in its caress.

An old proverb associated with the daisy says that when you can put your foot on three daisies spring has come. If this is true spring has fully come to the fields of Ipsley and Beoley. Damp places show patches of celandines with their waxen yellow petals. The tiny bird's eye, or speedwell (Veronica), captures and reflects the blue of the sky. Black Thorne bushes seem heaped with snow, so intensely white are its flowers, and dandelions are scattered upon the grass.

The song of the skylark is like an instant silver bell, and the cuckoo's note, at first faint and distant, grows louder with repetition.

By the bridge over the river below Salts Hill, I glimpsed my first swallow of 1968 in the form of a fleeting shadow upon the water. Looking up quickly I was delighted to see three of these eagerly awaited birds.

In a field under the grey walls of Ipsley Church, sheep and lambs nibbled on succulent grasses. The rooks on Beoley Hill maintained their raucous clamour, with ceaseless short flights around the tree tops, for no apparent reason other than the sheer joy of flying in the sunshine. Sometimes only two or three birds were airborne, then twenty or thirty pairs of black wings cleaved the air or floated lazily with the wind.

In arable fields the young wheat stretched in serpentine rows, four inches apart, between countless stones. These stones were smoothed and rounded by glacial action millions of years ago, when the earth trembled beneath the heavy tread of great beasts, whose horrid cries would have rent the primeval air.

Beoley is well named. The Normans called it "beau lieu", and it is indeed a beautiful place.

1968

Skylark RSPB breeding decline long term BDp2**Red status**

Rook RSPB Green Status *(Ref App F)*

*St Leonard's Church, Beoley (Ref App G)

PITCHEROAK WOOD

This is an age of planning and uniformity and/or experts and specialists in many spheres, but let us not overlook local knowledge and common sense.

*Pitcheroak is a natural deciduous wood in which the Oak is the dominant tree, with a mixture of birch, wild cherry, hazel, hawthorn and holly. Among these native trees the only "foreigners" are the Spanish Chestnuts, which I am told were planted to provide food for game birds when the land was part of the **Plymouth Estate.

The canopy of such a wood admits plenty of rain and sunlight, and in the undergrowth, of bramble, briar and bracken, can be seen many delightful wild flowers, each in its season contributing to the beauty and interest of this quiet place.

Guelder Rose © B Skeys.

There were also one or two specimens of the Guelder Rose, a shrub with an unusual flower, to which the pollinating insects are attracted by showy cream coloured florets, which are nothing more than sterile beacons, encircling the small fertile flowers.

In the autumn its translucent berries shone like rare blood-red jewels when lit by the rays of the setting sun.

Viburnum Opulus – Guelder Rose © B Skeys.

This shrub disappeared about four years ago (c1964) when the undergrowth was cleared by some indiscriminate forester.

But what have we now? Large areas of Pitcheroak Woods have been given over to close-planted evergreens – cypress and spruce, aliens to this countryside, which when mature will cast a gloomy pall upon the landscape and inhibit the wild flowers which now decorate the woodland floor. Little will grow in the shade of these trees and we shall look in vain for the violet anemone, bluebell and wild strawberry.

The Redditch Indicator 31st May 1968

*Conservation (Ref App. E)

**Estates belonging to the Earl of Plymouth

THRASHING A WALNUT TREE

"A woman, a dog and a Walnut tree, the more you thrash them, the better they be" goes the scurrilous old rhyme. Why a Walnut tree?

Roy Webb writes:
Further to the earlier answer, the purpose of thrashing a walnut tree was to increase the crop by shaking the pollen from the male flowers, at the top of the tree on to female flowers below.

Conservation (Ref App E)
9th October 1997

The Author writes:
I followed up this reply made by my brother with some further investigation. A friend found a similar old rhyme from the following source:

E Cobham Brewer 1810-1897, Dictionary of Phrase and Fable 1898.

It is said that the walnut tree thrives best if the nuts are beaten off with sticks and not gathered. Hence Fuller says, "Who, like a nut tree, must be manured by beating, or else would not bear fruit" (bk. ii. ch. 11). "A woman, a spaniel and a walnut tree the more you beat them the better they be."

Additional research reveals that the English walnut tree is self-pollinating (but not very efficiently), however, planting another tree nearby, with additional pollen carried by the wind will pollinate the flowers that were not fertilized and thus increase the crop. The tree should be fed with a good balanced fertilizer in late February. The nuts can be picked up off the ground or shaken off the tree.

And just one more comment about "thrashing". In knocking down the walnuts with a long pole, some branches are damaged. It seems that the damaged branches produce spurs which develop into fruit bearing flowers increasing the yield of the tree. Hence "the more you thrash them the better they be."

INFINITE PATIENCE OF NATURE

In an earlier letter to the Redditch Indicator I reflected on the infinite patience of *nature – ever ready to move in when man moves out. There is much evidence of this in those parts of old Redditch which have been cleared to await future development.

Grass and plantains (Plantago family), soon grow between the stones in abandoned entries and backyards, which the busy housewife, with mop and bucket, formerly kept in a state of antiseptic cleanliness. The mere absence of human footsteps around a house is the signal for a legion of plants to raise their un-bruised heads and for a time to soften these blighted areas with bright colours and symmetrical leaves.

Plenty of rough grass can be seen between rusty docks (Rumexobtusifolius) and dark green nettles. But the wild garden also displays in season, coltsfoot, daisies, bold stretches of golden dandelion, the cheerful ragwort, as much at home on broken walls as in patches of hard earth. The mallow with its delicate mauve petals and the pink balsam whose seed pods explode like miniature guns. Fireweed also called Rosebay Willow-herb, which used to decorate bomb sites in Birmingham, is also plentiful. The evening primrose is seen in some old gardens, where the yellow flowers assume a ghostly hue in the warm summer twilight.

One never ceases to marvel at the fecundity and persistence of nature. The Greeks expressed it far better in the legend of Proserpine. Where do the seeds of these plants come from? Many like dandelions and rosebay willow herb are wind-borne some are carried by animals and some perhaps on the wheels of vehicles. Countless seeds which have lain dormant beneath buildings and roads for many years, waiting to be released from their dark prison, are then nurtured by the twin agents of rain and sunshine. In previously cultivated areas many a weed which suffered annual decapitation now flourishes. A shriveled husk, having rested beneath the foundations of a house in which generations of people were born and went their way, now responds to an eternal dynamism, and a neglected thing of beauty will enjoy its brief hour upon the earth.

Grains of wheat taken from the tombs of the Pharaohs have sprouted ears of corn. How many Stone Age flowers give their sweetness to the Redditch air?

The Redditch Indicator – August 1977

*Nature (Ref Apps E and F) state of nature

RENEWAL

When sheep in sunlit stubbles move
On a quiet autumn day,
And leaves of oak and ash are falling
Gently in my way

Then the memory quietly turns
To early hopes by time annulled,
To high ambitions brought to nought
And youthful love that's unfulfilled.

So when the frost has strewn the leaves
The trees an austere beauty show,
Summer's garlands are all gone
But what remains is strong and true.

Undated

ADVENTUROUS WEEDS

In May the dandelion floats
On silken parachutes,
Later willow-herb and thistle,
And underground the couch-grass shoots.

Some seeds by birds are spread,
Others by wind and water borne,
And in the winter daisies flower
Upon the close–cropped lawn

Attack with shears or fork and hoe
All onslaughts they will brave,
Rake and burn, you cannot win
They'll grow upon your grave.

9th July 1977

CONSERVATION AND THE GREEN BELT, REDDITCH 1977

I am pleased to note that Redditch Development Corporation has been told by HM government to finish in five years, the job it was appointed to do, and then hand over to the elected District Council. I am also delighted that Birmingham City Council has been directed to look at its squalid inner suburbs and put its own house in order. Behind the city centre façade lie acres of deserted streets, with abandoned houses and derelict factories and warehouses.

Urban renewal in industrial cities is a sensible policy which, if adopted 20 years ago, would have spared pleasant parts of the countryside. Now is the time to confirm the Green Belt round Redditch, especially the vulnerable stretch between the town and Birmingham city boundary.

The Conservation Area of Alvechurch and Barnt Green should be extended eastward to include Lea End, Weatheroak and what is left of Wythall. This corner of north-east Worcestershire is scenically pleasant, and the Birmingham Architect's department has been nibbling away at it for years.

The Redditch Indicator 30th September 1977

Redditch Conservation Areas and Redditch Green Belt (Ref App. E) (Ref App F) state of nature

DETERMINING THE AGE OF AN ASH TREE

Three letters written between 15th May and 23rd May 2002 between the Arboricultural Officer, Redditch Borough Council and Roy Webb.

Arboriculture Officer
Redditch Borough Council
15th May 2002

Dear Mr Webb

With regard to your enquiry concerning the ash tree that has been felled at the rear of Allders department store in Redditch, I can report the following:

I inspected the remainder of the stump on 15th May 2002 and counted the annual growth rings of the tree to determine its age. After careful examination it appears that the tree was 103 years old.

I hope that this answers your enquiry, but should you have any further questions regarding the tree please do not hesitate to contact me.

Yours sincerely,

C. Walker

Arboriculture Officer

Trees, Conservation (Ref App E)

Greenfields
Redditch
19th May 2002

Dear Mr Walker

Thank you for your letter of May 15 and for counting the number of rings on the stump of the ash tree near Allders department store in Redditch.

It has occurred to me, that when a tree has stopped growing it does not produce any more of these rings, but it may continue to live for many years.

On Dodderhill Common near Droitwich there is a *stand of ancient oaks, a remnant of the forest of Feckenham. These protected trees stopped growing very many years ago, and Yosemite National Park in California, of course, is famous for its Sequoia Trees (**Red Wood Trees) which are upwards of 2,000 years old!

Which makes me think this Redditch ash tree may well have stood there for more than 103 years. I would appreciate your comments on this.

Yours sincerely,
Roy Webb

*stand = a group of small trees, Conservation (Ref App E)
** Red Wood trees (Ref App G)

Arboriculture Officer
Redditch Borough Council
23rd May 2002

Dear Mr Webb

Thank you for your recent letter regarding the age of the ash tree that was removed from land at the rear of Allders department store in Redditch. The age of a tree can be determined by counting the number of annual growth rings with each ring representing one year. The size of these rings can be influenced by climatic and environmental conditions as well as the age of the tree. A young tree in good growing conditions will produce a larger amount of annual growth than an over mature tree that may be in a state of decline. In the case of the latter the amount of annual growth produced may be negligible, but it will always produce an annual growth ring, which can be determined by careful visual examination, although it may appear that the overall size of the tree may not have increased.

I carefully examined the stump of the ash tree in question and counted the rings twice from different directions, from the edge to the centre, and on both occasions the number of annual rings was 103. It is therefore possible to say that 103 years is the actual age of the tree. I hope that this answers your questions.

Yours sincerely,

C. Walker

Arboriculture Officer

Conservation (Ref App. E)

A MAY EVENING – 1960

My brother with our mother.

One evening in May 1960 *(four years before the Development Corporation descended upon Redditch)* I strolled down Beoley Road over the Arrow Bridge and on to Beoley Mill Cottages with their latticed casements and colourful gardens. It was a perfect evening, the warm air full of the heady perfume from the May blossom, which festooned the lane side hedgerows. The sun was a vivid crimson disc. A gentle mist rose from the fields, from whose green depths the unseen cuckoo's note could be heard. About everything there was an air of new life, freshness and spring-time urgency. Nesting birds made rapid flights into the bushes, straws in their beaks, feverishly active at this busy time of the year. Waxy celandines lined the edges of damp ditches.

The roadside verges were bright with daisies, and other wild flowers, the most conspicuous being wild parsley (*Queen Anne's Lace*) stretching along the

Roy gathering flowers in the *lane.

hedgerows in Marlfield Lane to Icknield Street and on to Beoley Hill and its ancient church. Opposite Beoley Mill Cottages on this sunlit evening there was an old orchard and the trees standing in the tall lush grass of spring were a mass of blossom. A thrush which was perched on a pear tree was singing his heart out to the setting sun, whose blood-red rays bathed his speckled breast. The bird's throat throbbed with joy. He was, it seemed, worshipping the sun, whose warmth was filling him with vibrant life. To a professional naturalist this might seem to be an avian response to a natural stimulus. To me it was a moment of pure delight, which I shared with the bird in his abandoned ecstasy.

The old bridge has gone also Beoley Mill Cottages and most of the hedgerows. The once quiet *lane now reverberates to endless motor traffic.

That was the finest spring evening I can remember in seventy years of life.

These magic moments are rare and evanescent as the white clouds in the sky on a waking dream.

May 1991

*Marlfield Lane

Song Thrush RSPB Breeding decline long-term BDp2 **Red list** *(Ref App. F)*

GARDEN PESTS

Multitudinous insects now
The gardener's efforts bring to nought,
On either hand may be observed
The awful havoc they have wrought.

On seedling leaves of brassica
The beetle bites all day,
Nimble gymnasts on approaching
See them quickly fade away.
Wireworms tunnel in potatoes,
Blackfly swarm on runner beans,
Caterpillars, green and yellow,
Devour the tender winter greens.

Cats have scattered all the peas,
Then rend the night with horrid song,
Lettuce plants are decimated
By slugs six inches long.
Greenfly armies, slowly moving
On sticky leg and mealy wing,
Silent masses, surging onward
Envelop every living thing.

*Caterpillar of Mullein Moth on
Verbascum © B Skeys.*

The gardener's heart is black with fury
Against a score of foes,
And his anger as he fights them
No abatement knows.
But when small apples disappear,
He hesitates a while,
And as the culprit looks up shyly,
He's vanquished by a smile.

Undated.

CHANGES – BIRDS, FAUNA AND FLORA

It is interesting to reflect on some of the changes seen to birds, fauna and flora that have occurred in recent years – much of it is due to reshaping of the environment.

One loss is the disappearance of the peewit from many of its haunts. The development of arable land robbed this attractive bird of its feeding places.

Swifts are less numerous, and it is a long time since I saw a swallow; strangely enough, the last pair I saw had built their nest on the wall of the Danilo (*Essoldo*) cinema.

Frogs and toads have been decimated. Thousands of their young are destroyed every spring when attempting to cross the busy roads after leaving their spawning ponds.

Badgers, once numerous in the Church Hill area, with setts in the old *Marl Pits have retired from the scene.

Old meadows have been ploughed up which has reduced the number of primroses and cowslips. Countless mature trees have been felled – although a few have survived. On the credit side of the accounts, Arrow Valley Lake has provided a home for some interesting aquatic birds for example, Canada Geese.

The attractive little hawk, the kestrel, has been seen hovering over grass verges alongside the new roads and since the war, that showy wild flower the Himalayan Balsam (touch-me-not) with its explosive seed capsules has colonized the river banks.

The Redditch Advertiser 30th January 1992

*Marl: A fine ground sedimentary rock consisting of clay minerals, calcite or aragonite and silt, used as fertilizer

Swift RSPB Amber Status (Ref App F)

Frogs and Toads: endangered species (Ref App E and F) Ref state of nature

FATE OF RED SQUIRRELS

That attractive little animal, the red squirrel is no longer seen in these parts having been displaced by the grey squirrel, which is all too common, and can be a destructive pest. This alien "tree rat" was introduced from North America to the Duke of Bedford's Park at Woburn Abbey, whence it escaped, bred prolifically and spread throughout the country.

North American White Tipped, Gray squirrel. © E. F. Vozenilek, 2011.

The native *red squirrel is now mainly confined to the westerly parts of the United Kingdom.

I remember strolling across the fields to Gorcott Hill, in search of primroses, when we were delighted to see a red squirrel perched on a gate post, whilst behind him a few yards inside the wood, a fox in his glossy winter coat moved gracefully between the larch trees, so green in the spring after their winter bareness.

In 1943 on the Lickeys (*Lickey Hills*) a red squirrel descended a tree and sat on the end of the bench where I was sitting deep in thought. It was quite tame, having been fed, I expect, by visitors to the hills.

The arboreal (*tree*) squirrel will move on the ground in search of food, but never ventures far from the trees.

At home in the branches, they will jump from tree to tree but do occasionally miss their footing and fall to the ground.

One day at Mappleborough Green, I found one dying in the road, beneath tall trees from which it must have tumbled a few minutes earlier.

Its body was still warm, the tail twitched but it was dead.

The Redditch Advertiser 5th July 1992

*The *Red squirrel is a protected species in the UK (Ref App F)* state of nature

NATURE'S WAY

I never cease to marvel at the ability of wild plants to survive in an unfavourable environment. I have seen a small tree growing on the roof of a derelict Redditch factory, having rooted itself in the chimney pot. And I recently examined an old wall in Ipsley Street where the ivy-leaved toad-flax, growing from the pavement's edge, has climbed up the brickwork.

I have read that *Krakatoa, torn apart by a cataclysmic eruption which obliterated everything, after the lapse of a few years, was teeming with plant and animal life.

Nature abhors a vacuum and would survive the nuclear holocaust that everyone fears today.

The Redditch Advertiser 10th June 1998

When the volcano Krakatoa erupted (Ref App. G)

Conservation (Ref App. E) (Ref App. F) state of nature

THE DANDELION

Dandelion © E Moore.

"A golden galaxy of miniature suns,
fallen on the new spring grass."

New Millennium

CATCHING THISTLEDOWN

Thistle flowers © B Skeys.

There are fairies in the town,
In showers of thistledown,
They float elusive in the sun
On wings of gossamer spun

To catch them you may try,
But they twirl away on high,
This one a moment lingers
Then mocks my clumsy fingers,
Goes dancing lightly on
And with the breeze – is gone.

Undated

GLOW WORMS, SPERNAL 1940

Sixty years ago as I recall
In the cool of the evening,
At the day's ending
The sun's rays declining
Night was descending,
Its grey mantle falling
A pale moon ascending
And nature seemed sleeping

When lo the grass verges
With small lamps were shining,
As glow worms were climbing
A myriad green stems,
This magic display in early May
Remains in my mind today.

October 2000

Glow worm – Conservation (Ref App. E) (Ref App. F) state of nature

THE TRUTH OF THE MATTER

When sheep in sunlit stubbles move
On a quiet autumn day,
And leaves of oak and ash are falling
Gently in my way,
Then the memory quietly turns
To early hopes by time annulled,
To high ambitions brought to nought,
And youthful love that's unfulfilled.
But when the frost has strewn the leaves
The trees an austere beauty show,
Summer's garlands are all gone
And what remains is strong and true.

Undated

A WINTER SUNSET

"There is nothing more musical than a sunset. He who feels what he sees will find no more beautiful example of development in all that book which, alas, musicians read but too little – the book of Nature."

Claude Debussy (22.08.1862 – 25.03.1918)

I remember a village six miles south of Stratford-Upon-Avon (Ettington) from which was seen an awe-inspiring sunset on a frosty, bitingly cold December afternoon which was the shortest day of the year. It was a bleak cheerless day of leafless hedgerows, bare trees and a grey landscape, at the mercy of a killing wind. No colour in the countryside, but the sky was full of vivid hues. All the colours in the spectrum were mingled in that palette. A magnificent much enlarged sun slowly sank in all its grandeur into a fiery cavern in the western sky. The golden shafts shot upwards.

I realised why primitive men worshiped the sun. This powerful, flaming god, whose kingdom is in the heavens and the earth beneath, filled me with something akin to fear. I would fain have sunk to my knee in that cold Warwickshire lane, to pay homage to the lord of light and life.

Goldicote Manor, fronting the road was bathed in a golden light. The windows seemed aflame until the sun went down and the house resumed its dull aspect. As the sun descended there appeared a slim crescent moon like a slice of crystallised lemon and a few small scintillating stars.

The meteorologist would attribute this *phenomenon to diffraction of the sun's rays in an atmosphere highly charged with frost crystals. To me it was an unforgettable display of beauty and magic.

Undated

*The author recommends Robert Greenler, "Rainbows, Halos and Glories" (Ref App. I)

Chapter 10

Epilogue

"Keep close to nature's heart… and break clear away, once in a while, and climb a mountain or spend a week in the woods. Wash your spirit clean. None of nature's landscapes are ugly so long as they are wild."

John Muir (21.04.1838 – 24.12.1914)

In this manuscript you have been able to witness Roy Webb's life in all its stages. He was part of a family that has a long history in the Midland counties of Worcestershire and Warwickshire, England.

When old communities for one reason or another are developed, new residents do not have the opportunity to have a sense and feel of the lifestyle, nor of the natural environment of those people who lived there before them. These same people – men, women and their children, loved, laughed, worked and made their local town or village unique to them.

Roy, who died 31 January 2005, left us with his history of Redditch together with the love of its surrounding countryside. As he would have said, "I hope these little tidbits will help you to appreciate the 'old' Redditch which I so enjoyed."

Tina E Webb-Moore

Addendum

THE LIFE OF ELLEN ELIZABETH GAZEY
(Grandmother Gazey)

FOREWORD

You will have read in Chapter 2, my brother's letter to the Redditch Indicator (26th September 1991) about Grandmother Gazey (Ellen Elizabeth Gazey) and her anger at the small boys throwing stones at her ducks, and the reply by Patricia Heming her great granddaughter (12th December 1991).

The following information is the result of considerable help by Patricia Heming, who supplied further details about her great grandmother Ellen Elizabeth Gazey and her family, and also generously allowed me to include copies of family photographs.

HISTORY

Ellen Elizabeth Silvester (Grandmother Gazey), was born in 1860 at Cold Comfort Farm, Clifford Chambers, Gloucestershire and died in Redditch in 1943. She was the daughter of William Silvester of Cold Comfort Farm, and his wife Emma nee Hanson of The New Inn, Rowington, Warwickshire. Ellen married Walter George Gazey of Weston-Sub-Edge, Gloucestershire, in 1879 when she was 19 and Walter was 20. With the exception of Frederick William who was born in Redhill, Alcester, Warwickshire, their children were born at the ***Toll House, which stood at the junction of Birmingham Road, and Bordesley Lane, Redditch, and was known as "Granny Locke's". At that time Walter worked at Bordesley Lodge Farm on land which was once part of Bordesley Abbey.

When Walter died of a heart attack in January 1901, they were living at 253 Beoley Road, Redditch. They had five children who survived to adulthood and one who died as a newborn (name unknown).

ELLEN AND WALTER'S CHILDREN

Frederick William born Oct 1883, (died June 1968) married Ethel Eades 1938 – no offspring.

Frederick William lived in Keeper's Cottage, Oversley, Alcester. He died in 1968 when an unknown well collapsed in his home and he drowned.
*(****Francis Frith, Warwickshire Memories)*

Joseph George born 04.11.1887 (died 1969) married Amy Knight 1917, they had two sons, Edward born 1918 and Gerald born 1927.

Ellen Elizabeth Anne born 21.11.1890 (died 1970) married James Ellins 1916.
James Ellins killed at the Battle of the Somme (WWI) 1918 – no offspring.

Thomas Henry born 1893 (died 11.03.1948) married Cissy Robinson January 1920 they had two children: Thomas Henry born November 1920 and Mary Kathleen born 05.07.1924, (died 02.02.1995).

Sarah Jane born 16.04.1895 Spinster (died 1977).

***THOMAS HENRY'S DAUGHTER** Mary Kathleen Gazey and **GRANDDAUGHTER** Patricia Mary Dyer,* **see family history below:**
Mary Kathleen Gazey married Cyril John Dyer, 24.12.1945 they had two children Patricia Mary Born 20.08.1948 and Peter John born 10.10.1960.

Patricia Mary Dyer married Barry John Heming 09.01.1971 at St Leonard's Church, Beoley – no offspring.

Patricia Heming's great great grandfather W Martin James, owned the fishing tackle factory at 75 Beoley Road. Martin's daughter married John Dyer (Patricia's great grandfather) who had a hardware shop in Alcester Street, Redditch.

This photograph taken in the garden of 253 Beoley Road, shows Sarah Jane (Jin) with her hands on the shoulders of Mary Kathleen, with Mary's brother Tom on her right and Ellen Elizabeth Anne (Nell) standing behind him.

ELLEN ELIZABETH GAZEY
LIFE WITH A FARM AND FIVE CHILDREN

Last known photograph of Ellen Elizabeth Gazey circa 1940/42 with her dogs Lassie the Old English Sheep dog on the left and Tangee the Terrier on the right.

Farm and Home Management

If Ellen Elizabeth was alive today she would have a story to tell that might put many women to shame. We have to admire her courage, at the age of 41 she became a widow with five children to look after. She did not have, nor I expect even if it had been available to her, would she have accepted government "benefits". We will see that she made it her responsibility to look after her children undaunted – feeding, clothing, and educating her children and at the same time tending and looking after all the animals and poultry on her small farm.

The expression on her face in all her photographs is impenetrable, but we should look much further than this. She never has her hair out of place, her apron is white, (a "Sunday apron" which she made herself) her boots tightly laced, here is a woman who at all times and in spite of all her hardship was in control.

The *photograph of Ellen, with her sheep and dog is taken in one of her fields. She had two fields, "Gazey Fields" where she kept three or four milking

"Dol" standing at the junction of 223 Beoley Road and Prospect Road where Joseph George Gazey lived (undated).

cows, several sheep and poultry. These same fields were bounded by the **River Arrow which came through the meadows at Bordesley (Abbey Meadows) took a right hand turn towards Beoley Mill Cottages, then a left and then right where it crossed the bottom of Beoley Road and was referred to as Beoley Brook. The river was to claim the life of her carthorse "Dol" who slipped into the waters and was drowned.

Wading Through the Waters of the Brook (River Arrow)

In earlier years when the water was high and there was no bridge over The Brook, Ellen waded waist deep in the water to reach her fields. Imagine her trudging through the brook, water dripping from her skirts, shoes and stockings wet through on a bitingly cold winter's day, to walk on to the fields and feed the animals and poultry. Then on her return journey to walk again through the brook, arriving home with wet skirts clinging to her legs and her hands freezing cold. She would dry her wet skirts, and stand in front of the fire

Children playing in the waters of The Brook (River Arrow) at the bottom of Beoley Road, Redditch (undated).

with her hands and body slowly warming, her children waiting to have their meal, and the dog watching by the hearth.

Ellen's Garden

Ellen Elizabeth Gazey with her grandsons: Edward (Ted) on the right and Gerald (sons of Joseph George) with her ducklings circa 1930/31.

Ellen's Husbandry

The garden at the back of 253 Beoley Road, was the centre of Ellen's husbandry, housing a small dairy where she would make butter. The milk from her cows was placed in a churn and prepared for local delivery on a cart. Many garden tools were to be found in the shed. The garden was also the home for all of Ellen's young animals and poultry that needed special help, ducklings, young chickens and lambs were all nurtured and taken care of until they were strong enough to go into the field. Later in the year pheasants, geese, turkeys and cockerels were hung in the shed in readiness for sale at the Christmas Market.

Ellen and Her Daughters

After World War I Ellen was joined by her daughter Ellen Elizabeth Anne known as Nell, and her other daughter Sarah Jane, known as Jin. Not only did they keep the small farm, but as we read in Patricia Heming's ***** letter in reply to my brother, they looked after a large allotment at the back of Sillins Avenue, growing vegetables and keeping pigs from which they produced bacon. With a further allotment at the back of Redditch High School down Lady Harriet's Lane, they grew soft fruits, apples and pears. All this produce together with eggs from the chickens could be bought from Ellen and her daughters. A notice in the front window of 253 Beoley Road, invited would be buyers to knock on the door for assistance. They had in fact a small "Cottage Industry", with all the produce organically grown and freshly picked. What else could anyone wish for?

A Farmer's Daughter

Ellen the daughter of a farmer, remained so all her life her strength and courage knew no bounds.

Family Pride

Ellen is remembered with pride by her family. Would she want to be remembered forever through this book? I hope so. Let's raise our glasses to Ellen and her life.

*	Photograph of Ellen (Ref Chapter 2)
**	River Arrow (Ref "Ordnance Survey" Map dated 1887)
***	Toll House (Ref Appendix G)
****	Francis Frith, (Warwickshire Memories) (Ref App I)
*****	Letter from Patricia Heming to Roy Webb (Ref Chapter 2)

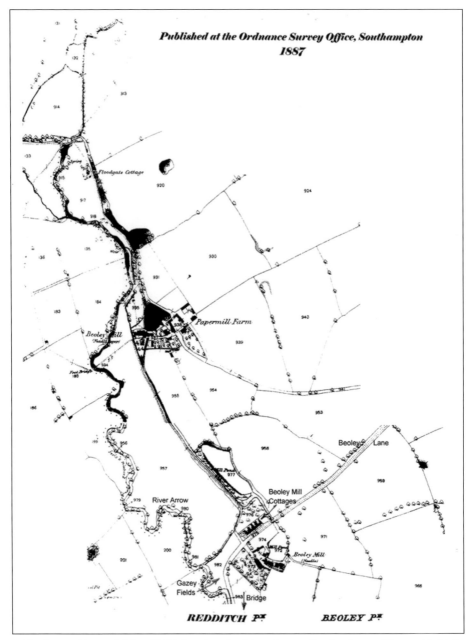

"Ordnance Survey" Map 1887 showing the River Arrow, Beoley Lane, "Gazey Fields" and Beoley Mill Cottages, Redditch. Courtesy of Forge Mill Needle Museum, Redditch, Worcestershire, England.

List of Appendices

APPENDIX A

COMMON ALDER

Common Alder is a common tree of riversides, fens and wet woodlands. The exposed roots of riverside Common Alders provide fish with shelter from predators or high flows, and their leaves provide food for invertebrates such as the larvae of caddis flies, stoneflies and water beetles. These, in turn, are preyed upon by fish including Salmon and Brown Trout. The wood of Common Alder does not rot under water, so was historically used for shoring-up canals and riverbanks. It was also used to make charcoal and clogs!

How to identify

Alder has both male and female flowers – long, yellow-brown catkins and small, red 'cones' that ripen and harden when pollinated. Alder is easily recognised by the combination of habitat, rounded leaves and purplish buds.

Where to find it

Widespread.

ALDER BUCKTHORN

Alder Buckthorn is a small, thorn-less tree of wet woodland, riverbanks and heathlands. It is widespread, but scarce, across England and Wales. Clusters of pale green flowers appear in late spring and bunches of red berries ripen to a purple-black colour in autumn. Both Alder and Purging Buckthorn are the main food plants of the Brimstone Butterfly.

How to identify

A close relative of Purging Buckthorn, Alder Buckthorn can be distinguished by its narrower leaves with wavy margins and rounded tips, as well as its red (turning purple) berries.

Where to find it

Wide spread in England and Wales.

Information about the Alder: by kind permission of **Worcestershire Wildlife Trust**

Worcestershire Wildlife Trust is the foremost organisation actively restoring and protecting wildlife and wild places in Worcestershire. The Trust owns and manages over 70 nature reserves throughout the county and works with local community members and other organizations to encourage a landscape for people and wildlife. It has around 20,000 members and around 450 volunteers who support the Trust by active involvement in its conservation, education, fundraising and administration work. More information can be found on http://www.worcswildlifetrust.co.uk/who-we-are

Author's Note: The above information current Summer 2013

APPENDIX B

NATIONAL CHARACTER AREAS (NCA)

National Character Areas (NCAs) divide England into 159 distinct natural areas. Arden is NCA97

ARDEN

"Arden comprises farmland and former wood-pasture lying to the south and east of Birmingham, including part of the West Midlands conurbation. Traditionally regarded as the land lying between the River Tame and the River Avon in Warwickshire, the Arden landscape also extends into north Worcestershire to abut the Severn and Avon Vales. To the north and north-east it drops down to the open landscape of the Mease/Sence Lowlands. The eastern part of the NCA abuts and surrounds Coventry, with the fringes of Warwick and Stratford-upon-Avon to the south."

www.naturalengland.org.uk

Published with permission of Natural England Open Government Licence (NE OGL).

APPENDIX C

COVENTRY CATHEDRAL

Through the generosity of Robert Orland owner/creator etc. of Historic Coventry (www.historiccoventry.co.uk) I was able to include photographs of the cathedral, Rob also gave his permission for me to include some of the text below to give insight into the night of the blitz of Coventry which took place in 1940. Note that text is subject to copyright and may not be reproduced without permission.

"The first warning locally that a raid was about to strike was just ten minutes before 7 o'clock when our anti-aircraft defence team were told that bombers were heading for Coventry. At 7:10 pm the siren sounded,

and just as the sound of the siren died down, the first showers of incendiaries were already raining down from the path-finding Heinkel 111's above. It was remarked by some that it was an early start that evening... it was going to be a very late finish."

About the cathedral that was destroyed and the design of the new cathedral:

St Michael's ruins, Place No.18

"As we're in the area, I couldn't resist revisiting our favourite old building again for a triple photo helping! It's sobering to think that in the hands of a less sympathetic architect, all this could have been lost forever... the committee for the rebuilding of Coventry Cathedral only stipulated that the tower, its spire and perhaps the south porch be kept.

Very fortunately for us all, Basil Spence (later to be given a Knighthood) had a 'vision' on his first ever visit to the ruins. Like the Provost during the war, he saw a beauty in the surviving burnt out shell, and knew instantly that he could never destroy what remained. As he stood there, looking through the north windows towards the ground being reserved for any possible future building he envisaged an altar with a great picture of Christ behind it – seen through the bodies of saints. This of course turned out to be the huge tapestry seen through the Great West Screen of Saints and Angels. To use his words: '…the new Cathedral should grow from the old and be incomplete without it'."

The Coventry Litany of Reconciliation is prayed in the new Cathedral every weekday at noon (in the ruins on Fridays) and is used throughout the world by the Community of the Cross of Nails.

Coventry Litany of Reconciliation – Coventry Cathedral
www.coventrycathedral.org.uk/...reconciliation.../coventry-litany-of-rec...

APPENDIX D

HANLEY SWAN, MALVERN, WORCESTERSHIRE
Hanley Swan www.hanleyswanpond.co.uk

Author's Note: This beautiful village has its own school, church, village hall, village pub, pond and butcher. It is blessed with a supportive and happy community. A well-known resident and gardener, Brian Skeys kindly gave his permission to use many of his photographs of flowers, trees and birds. His granddaughters Rebecca and Louise also gave their permission to include their pictures for "The Art Class".

Brian Skeys
Chairman
The Black Pear Gardening Club in Worcestershire
www.blackpeargc.org.uk

APPENDIX E

REDDITCH CONSERVATION AREAS AND GREEN BELT
The following information is published with the kind permission of Redditch and Bromsgrove Councils. With special thanks to Charlotte Wood, Planning Administrative Assistant, Redditch Borough Council and her colleagues.

Redditch Conservation Areas
Policy B (NE) 10a, Sites of National Wildlife Importance:

> *"There are currently no sites of international wildlife importance within the Borough of Redditch. However, of great importance are sites of national wildlife importance. The concept of Sites of Special Specific*

Interest (SSSIs) and National Nature Reserves (NNRs) was introduced in the National parks and Access to the Countryside Act 1949. The protection of SSSIs was greatly increased by the Wildlife and Countryside Act 1981 and the Wildlife and Countryside (Amendment) Act 1985. Currently there are six Sites of Special Specific Interest (SSSIs) in the borough of Redditch, which cover a range of different habitats:"

Dagnell End Meadow
Ipsley Alders Marsh
Rookery Cottage Meadows
Rough Hill and Wirehill Woods
Trickses Hole
Wylde Moor, Feckenham

Policy B (NE)10b, Sites of Regional or Local Wildlife Importance:

"Local Nature reserves are declared by Local Authorities under the National Parks and Access to the Countryside Act 1949 and are statutorily protected sites. Local Nature Reserves in Redditch are:"

Pitcheroak Wood
Foxlydiate Wood
Walkwood Coppice
Southcrest Wood
Oakenshaw Wood
Proctors Barn Meadows

Planning Policy Guidance 9 (PPG9) (Nature Conservation)

"Also stresses the importance for nature conservation of sites with no statutory designation. This includes Special Wildlife Sites (SWS). There are a number of these in the Borough of Redditch; these are:"

Abbey & Forge Mill Pools and Streams
Arrow Valley Lake
Berrow Hill
Bow, Shell, Swans & Seeley Brooks

Brandon Brook Meadow
Brookhouse Meadows & Feckenham Bank
Brooks Coppice & Wheatfield Coppice
Burial Lane
Dagnell Brook
Downsell Woods
Foxlydiate & Pitcheroak Woods
Lady's Coppice & Martin Bank
Lodge Pool
Mill Coppice
New Coppice
Oakenshaw Fenny Rough
Oakenshaw Spinney
Oakenshaw Wood
Pitcher Oak Golf Course
Old Rectory Meadow
Ravensbank Drive Bridle Track
River Arrow Papermill and Beoley Mill Ponds and Stream
Shurnock Meadows
Southcrest Wood
The Rough
Walkwood Coppice

Redditch Green Belt

"For current information please visit:
Redditch's Local Plan No.3
policy/development-plan/local-plan-no3.aspx#localplan3

> *Where you will find an excellent map – 'proposals map (high resolution)'*
> *PDF (further down the page) which illustrates all the Green Belt land*
> *that currently lies within Redditch Borough. This Plan was adopted in*
> *May 2006. I also would like to draw to your attention that the Planning*
> *Team is currently preparing the Local Plan No 4. The draft publication*
> *of this is now available to read on our website alongside the draft policies*
> *map, you can view both of these using the links below. The changes you*
> *will see to the green belt on the proposals map are in Brockhill and also*
> *a small area in Foxlydiate. At present these proposals are only in draft*

form and so are subject to possible changes until this version of the Local Plan is adopted."

http://redditch.whub.org.uk/cms/environment-and-planning/planning-services/planning-policy/development-plan/emerging-local-plan-no4.aspx
Link to map:
http://www.redditchbc.gov.uk/KeyDocuments/PDF/LP4%20Policies%20Map.pdf
Author's Note: The above information current 2013

CONSERVATION AROUND THE WORLD

(A small list from the many conservation sites around the world.)
Europe Nature Conservation, Environment Issues | The Nature ...
www.nature.org › Where We Work › Regions
United States Nature Conservation, Environment Issues | The ...
www.nature.org › Where We Work › Regions › North America
History of **Audubon** and Waterbird Conservation | National Audubon...
birds.audubon.org/history-audubon-and-waterbird-conservation
Australia Nature Conservation, Environment Issues | The Nature ...
www.nature.org › Where We Work
Pacific Islands – **Conservation** International
www.conservation.org › ... › Asia-Pacific › Pacific Islands
China Nature **Conservation**, Environment Issues | The Nature ...
www.nature.org/ourinitiatives/regions/asiaandthepacific/china/index.
Latin **America** – Where We Work – Wildlife **Conservation** Society ...
www.wcs.org › Where We Work
African Conservation Foundation
www.africanconservation.org/APPENDIX F

APPENDIX F

ROYAL SOCIETY FOR THE PROTECTION OF BIRDS (RSPB)
All the information referencing the RSPB is by kind permission of Andrew Waters, RSPB Communications Officer, Midlands Region, Oxfordshire. Andrew has been unstinting in his support. I also would like to thank Ray Kennedy, Richard Newton, Andy Hay, and all of the RSPB photographers for their delightful photographs which I am permitted to use.

BIRDS OF CONSERVATION CONCERN (BOCC)

The RSPB uses a red, amber and green list, to classify birds that are under threat. Since the last review in 2002 they state:

- *"A total of 246 species have been assessed against a set of objective criteria to place each on one of three lists – green, amber and red – indicating an increasing level of conservation concern.*
- *There are 52 species on the red list, 126 on the amber list and 68 on the green list. The red list has increased by 12 since 2002, with 18 species added but six moved from red to amber. Eleven species are now on the red list due to an important change in criteria since the last assessment."*

Author's Note:

In addition there are a total of 30 birds which have **Red status** which are also classified as "breeding decline long-term", BDp2. Where applicable I have defined the status of each bird in the book content. Additional information can be found on:

Birds of conservation concern 3 2009 – RSPB

www.rspb.org.uk/Images/BoCC_tcm9-217852.pdf

Question: How can I help?

Answers: a) Go to State of Nature to see how you can **Get Involved**

b) Give Nature a Home

STATE OF NATURE
www.rspb.org.uk/state of nature
Report with introduction by Sir David Attenborough

This report is a collaboration between *25 UK conservation and research organizations see *www.rspb.org.uk/stateofnature*

The report discusses the effects of the environment on each part of the UK, together with information about the UK's 14 Overseas Territories (UKOTs) around the world.

*Conservation and Research Organizations working together:
Amphibian & Reptile Conservation
Association of British Fungus Groups

British Lichen Society
British Mycological Society
British Trust for Ornithology
Buglife
Butterfly Conservation
Conchological Society of Great Britain and Ireland
Marine Conservation Society
National Biodiversity Network
People's Trust for Endangered Species
Plant Life
Pond Conservation
Rothampstead Research
Royal Botanical Gardens, Kew
The Bat Conservation Trust
The Biological Records Centre/Centre for Ecology and Hydrology
The Botanical Society of the British Isles
The British Bryological Society
The Bumblebee Conservation Trust
The Mammal Society
The Marine Biological Association
The Wildfowl and Wetlands Trusts
The Wildlife Trusts

GIVE NATURE A HOME

Inspiring the nation to give nature a home:
rspb.org.uk/homes

Habitat and Feeding: Yellow Hammer, Redwing, Fieldfare and Song Thrush classified under RSPB breeding decline long-term BDp2**Red status**

The Yellow Hammer Priority Action

- Make sure there is a plentiful supply of seeds throughout the year, by considering unsprayed root crops, conversion of pasture to arable rotation set-aside wildlife cover crops and unsprayed cereal, rape and linseed.
- Make sure there is a plentiful supply of insects by leaving rough grass margins and not spraying root crops, cereal rape and linseed. © rspb

The Redwing is a winter bird and is the UK's smallest true thrush. It has a creamy strip above the eye and orange-red flank patches. Put out windfall apples and chopped fruit in your garden and this will encourage them to come to visit.

Where to see them

In open countryside it likes hedges and orchards as well as open, grassy fields. They will come to parks and gardens. Often joins with flocks of fieldfares.

When to see them

Migrants arrive from September, with most in October and November. They leave again in March and April, although occasionally birds stay later. ©RSPB

Fieldfares

Fieldfares are large, colourful thrushes, much like a mistle thrush in general size, shape and behaviour. They stand very upright and move forward with purposeful hops. They are very social birds, spending the winter in flocks of anything from a dozen or two to several hundred strong. These straggling, chuckling flocks that roam the UK's countryside are a delightful and attractive part of the winter scene. Windfall apples and chopped fruit will encourage them to feed in your garden.

Where to see them

Best looked for in the countryside, along hedges and in fields. Hawthorn hedges with berries are a favourite feeding area. In late winter grass fields, playing fields and arable fields with nearby trees and hedges are a favourite place. May come into gardens in severe winters when snow covers the countryside.

When to see them

They begin to arrive from October and numbers build up as the winter progresses. Birds start to return in March and some may stay into May.

What they eat

Insects, worms and berries.

Song Thrush

The song thrush is associated with thick hedgerows, native woodland and damp ground, especially grazed pasture.

The UK song thrush population fell by 59% between 1970 and 1998*.

Loss of food-rich habitats, particularly in the summer, is thought to be the main cause of the decline on farmland.

*Data source: British Trust for Ornithology

This information is updated every year and the latest Song Thrush page is: http://blx1.bto.org/birdtrends/species.jsp?s=sonth&year=2012

Key points

Maintain or restore damp areas of grazed pasture or woodland – damp habitats through the summer are essential for chick survival.

Avoid management of hedgerows between March and August to protect nesting after the berry crop has been taken.

Author's note: The above information current September 2013

APPENDIX G

RESEARCH SOURCES (See individual titles below for information.)

Airship

Black Country Bugle (re siting the Air Ship) *www.blackcountrybugle.co.uk*

Archaeology

The Archaeology of Redditch New Town – Redditch Borough Council *www.redditchbc.gov.uk/*

Archive and Archaeology – Worcestershire County Council *www.worcestershire.gov.uk/cms/archive-and-archaeology*

Bat-fowling

Bat-fowling – definition of Bat-fowling by the Free Online Dictionary... *www.thefreedictionary.com/Bat-fowling*

Bee Keepers

* "The British Beekeepers Association (BBKA) works to promote bees and... dependent on pollination at a time when a crisis is threatening the world's honey bees."

British Beekeepers Association (BBKA) *www.bbka.org.uk/*

Worcestershire Beekeepers *www.wbka.net/*

Bordesley Abbey
Houses of Cistercian monks – Abbey of Bordesley: A History of the ...
www.british-history.ac.uk/report.aspx?compid=36474

Biodiversity
Biodiversity – Redditch Borough Council – Worcestershire Hub
redditch.whub.org.uk

Biodiversity – Worcestershire
www.worcestershire.gov.uk/cms/biodiversity.aspx

Blitz of Birmingham
1940 – Diary of a *Birmingham* schoolboy – Brian David Williams
brianwilliams.org.uk/diary/1940.html

Blitz of Coventry
Rob Orland's Historic **Coventry**
www.historiccoventry.co.uk/gb/gb.ph

Cigarette Cards
Cigarette Cards and Trade Cards collectors site – History of Tobacco ...
www.cigarettecards.co.uk/intro.htm

Glow-worm
BBC Nature – Common glow-worm videos, news and facts *www.bbc.co.uk*
Icknield Street

Icknield Street
Icknield Street | Learn everything there is to know about Icknield...
www.reference.com/browse/icknield+street

Krakatoa, Indonesia
When the volcano Krakatoa erupted in 1883 it made ... – OMG Facts
www.omg-facts.com › Technology Facts

Listed Buildings *(A selection.)*

Church of St George Grade II, St George's Road, Redditch, Worcestershire
redditch.whub.org.uk

Church of St Peter – Coughton – British Listed Buildings
www.britishlistedbuildings.co.uk/en-305309-church-of-st-peter-coughto...

Coughton Court
www.coughtoncourt.co.uk/

English Heritage Home Page | English Heritage
www.english-heritage.org.uk/

National Trust
www.nationaltrust.org.uk/

Norgrove Court – British Listed Buildings
www.britishlistedbuildings.co.uk/en-156611-norgrove-court-feckenham...

St Leonard's Church, Beoley, Church Hill and Abbey Park
www.stleonardsbeoley.org.uk

Listed Buildings in Redditch, Worcestershire, England | British Listed ...
www.britishlistedbuildings.co.uk/england/worcestershire/redditch

Worcester Cathedral
www.worcestercathedral.co.uk/

Liturgy
Alternative Services Series 3 – Oremus
www.oremus.org/liturgy/series3/

Manorial Rights and Lordships
The Hubands of Ipsley – Huband Family and Ancestry
hubandfamily.com/ipsley.html

Manorial Handlists History of Manorial Documents –Worcestershire
worcestershire.whub.org.uk/cms/pdf/RecordsIndex-ManorialHandlist.pdf
Lordships – Msgb.co.uk – Manorial Society of Great Britain
www.msgb.co.uk/lordships.html

Military
BBC ON THIS DAY | 15 | 1940: Victory for RAF in Battle of Britain
www.bbc.co.uk/onthisday/hi/dates/stories/september/15/.../3521611.stm

Military Medal – A Multimedia History of World War One
www.firstworldwar.com/atoz/militarymedal.htm

Rolls of Honour
Details extracted from, and used with permission
www.roll-of-honour.com

Royal Military School of Music – British Army Website
www.army.mod.uk/music/23271.aspx

Worcestershire Regiment (29th/36th of Foot)
www.worcestershireregiment.com

World War One executions – History Learning Site
www.historylearningsite.co.uk/world

Nurses without Caps Florence Nightingale
Foundation *www.florence-nightingale-foundation.org.uk/*

Nurse's caps introduced to help patients – Telegraph
www.telegraph.co.uk › Health › Health News

Redditch
Conservation Areas – Redditch Borough Council – Worcestershire Hub

The Palace Theatre, Alcester Street and Grove Street, Redditch
www.arthurlloyd.co.uk/RedditchTheatres

Palace Theatre, Redditch | Theatre Tickets, whats on and theatre
www.theatresonline.com/theatres/redditch-theatres/palace-theatre/index.html

Redditch Library – Worcestershire County Council
www.worcestershire.gov.uk/cms/library-services/.../redditch.aspx

Redditch for God local churches network website *www.redditchforgod.net/*

Red Wood Trees
Redwood Forest Facts – SaveTheRedwoods.org
www.savetheredwoods.org

Royal Societies
Royal Horticultural Society (RHS)
www.rhs.org.uk

Royal Society for the Protection of Cruelty to Animals (RSPCA)
www.rspca.org.uk

Royal Society for Protection of Birds
homes.rspb.org.uk

Victorian Crime and Punishment
Victorian Crime and Punishment from E2BN
vcp.e2bn.org

APPENDIX H

HISTORY SOCIETIES
(Small selection. Go to "Local history societies in Worcestershire" for more information.)

Feckenham Forest History Society Home Page
www.feckenham-forest-history-society.org.uk/home.html

Forge Mill Needle Museum and Bordesley Abbey Visitor Centre
www.forgemill.org.uk/

Redditchheritage.org.uk
www.redditchheritage.org.uk/

Redditch History
www.redditchhistory.com

History of Studley, Warwickshire
www.studleyparishcouncil.org.uk/history.html

Local history societies in Worcestershire: Local History Online
www.local-history.co.uk › Local history societies

Worcestershire Historical Society
www.worcestershirehistoricalsociety.co.uk/

APPENDIX I

Reading References:

Anstis, Gordon "Redditch: Success in the Heart of England – the History of Redditch New Town 1964-85" Published by Companies (PBC) (1985)

Author's Note: I would like to acknowledge the assistance of 'the Democratic Services Team at Bromsgrove District and Redditch Borough Councils' who referenced the book by Gordon Anstis.

Bovril The history of Bovril advertising; Bovril Limited, Peter Hadley...
www.amazon.com/The-history-Bovril-advertising-Limited/.../09501574...

Clews Roy Famous author from Redditch (From Redditch Advertiser)
www.redditchadvertiser.co.uk

Frith, Francis Warwickshire Memories, (see Frederick William Gazey by Patricia Heming)
www.francisfrith.com/uk

Greenler, Robert Rainbows, Halos, and Glories, Publisher: Cambridge University Press (26 January 1990)

Hancox E. and Mindykowski A., 2007, A Rapid Survey of the Area to the South of Beoley Castle, Redditch, Worcestershire County Council internal report

Hooke, D 1980 Studley Parish Survey Unpublished report held by Warwickshire Historic Environment Record

Richardson, R.H., 'The Administration of the Old Poor Law in Ipsley, 1797-1804' in *Studies in Worcestershire Local History Vol. 4* (1988**) edited by R.Whittaker**

APPENDIX J

Population figures for Redditch from 1921 to 2011
Census records reveal that the population for Redditch in 1921 was 22,100. In the year 2011 it had risen to 84,214.

Place of Birth	Population
All categories	84,214
Europe	81,263
Antartica + Oceania	72
The Americas and Caribbean	404
Middle East and Asia	2,022
Africa	453

By kind permission of: The Research & Intelligence Unit (Worcestershire County Council) Census data figures from ONS

Details of population movement within Worcestershire can be found on: www.worcestershire.gov.uk/cms/pdf/worcs_demographic_report_2005-100.pdf

APPENDIX K

UK Military Information:

Falkland War 1982 – war between Argentina and the United Kingdom
It is reported that in the 74 days of the war, 255 British servicemen and 3 female Falkland Island civilians were killed.
Iraq War 2003 – 2011: information found but not substantiated is 179 servicemen were killed as at 2011.

Afghanistan War – 2001 – present (2013) The Ministry of Defence figures at this time indicate a total of 444 British forces personnel or MOD civilians have died while serving in Afghanistan since the start of the war.

Author's Note: The above information current July 2013.

Index

red squirrels 131

Redditch, 1887 map 146

Redditch, 1960s development 13, 90, 102, 108, 123

Redditch Church of England school 12

Redditch churches 67, 68, 71, 74, 88

Redditch County High School 37, 95

"Redditch Indicator" 73, 93

Redditch market 46-7, 69

Redditch Society 88

River Arrow ("The Brook") 21, 23, 78, 143-4, 146: mills 79

Royal Warwickshire Regiment 39

Royal Worcestershire Regiment 39

S

Sambourne 4-5

Sheldon family 75

Shelfield 102

shrubs 117-18

Sillins Avenue 145

The Slough, Studley 4, 111

Sly, D. 85

soldiers and families 36-8: Rolls of Honour 39

Southcrest 74

sparrow catching 27

squirrels 131

St George's Church, Redditch 68

St Leonard's Church, Beoley 56, 75, 81, 115

St Luke's First School 62

St Peter's Church, Ipsley 65, 66

St Stephen's Church, Redditch 67, 71

Studley 6-7, 111

Styler, Alf 37

Styler, James Henry and Henrietta 57-8

Styler, Prudence 47, 57, 69

Styler, Sydney 87

sunset 137

sweet sellers 12, 69

T

taxis 69

Temperance Hall 90

thrashing a walnut tree 111

"Tiger", the terrier dog 16

Toll House, Bordesley 25, 139

trees 43-4, 109, 117-19, 124-6, 148-9

"trolley problem" 48-50

W

"Wagon and Horses", Beoley Road 18

War Memorial 37

Washford Mill 79

water bailiff 19

Watery Lane 21

Watson, Tommy 37

Webb, Doreen 4

Webb, Florence E. 77

Webb, Irene Muriel 41, 62

Webb, Katrina 41

Webb, Mary 4

Webb, Roy

 Adventurous Weeds 122

 April Showers 112-13

 Bird Song in Springtime 96

 The Blue Tit 104